RAJBANSHI'S OF NEPAL

RAJBANSHI'S OF NEPAL

by

Dr. Rajesh Gautam

ADROIT

ADROIT PUBLISHERS

Published by
ADROIT PUBLISHERS
4675/21, Ganpati Bhawan, Ansari Road,
Daryaganj, New Delhi-110 002
Phones : 011-23266030, 55302465

Distributors
AKHIL BOOK DISTRIBUTORS
e-mail: akhilbooks@yahoo.com
akhilbooks@hotmail.com

ISBN : 81-87392-49-5

Layout
Sudhir Vatsa

Laser Typeset by
Arpit Printographers
E-mail: arpiprinto@yahoo.com

Printed in India on behalf of M/s Adroit Publishers by
Arpit Printographers, B-7, Saraswati Complex,
Subhash Chowk, Laxmi Nagar, Delhi-110 092
Phones : 09350809192, 30971860

Preface

Situated on the southern lap of the Himalayas, Nepal is a sovereign nation divided into three ecological and geographical zones: the plains (the terai) to the south, the hills (Mahabharat) in the central region and the Himalayas to the north. The Sherpas, Tamangs etc., which are culturally similar to the Tibetan people, inhibit in the northern part of Nepal which is almost a snowy region. The main inhabitants of the Mahabharat ranges are the Magars, Limbus, Gurungs, Sunuwars, Kirats, Newars, Bahuns, Chhetries etc., and the inhabitants of the Terai (which also includes inner-valleys) are the Tharus, Darais, Danuwars, Chepangs, Dhimals and so on. In addition, the Santhals, Rajbanshi's also reside here.

Diverse as it is, the natural setting of Nepal has also influenced the cultures, languages and other life-styles of the people residing in a specific area. The people residing in a particular region speak a different language and practice a different culture from those who reside in other regions. The geographical pattern has thus been a base of the conglomeration of the people who speak various languages; practice different cultures and adopt diverse lifestyles. Before the process of unification began in early 1700s, doubtlessly, all these people had not a common self and existence. No environment was created for these people to realise that the country was their common home and any problem in any part of the country would amount to be of their common concern. It was obvious for these Nepalese people, divided into various principalities then, to lack a feeling that they were the flowers blooming in a common garden.

After the emergence of the Great King Prithvi Narayan Shah the petit political borders began to fade away, and the people of different castes and cultures came to realise that they belonged to a common Nepali-caste as its various organs. However, this realisation-process suffered a setback when the Ranas took hold of the reign of governance. The Rana regime hindered the development of a healthy nationality and the co-ordination of inter-region peoples.

After the revolution of 2007 B.S., a change occurred in the required direction. These diverse peoples pledged themselves to move ahead for the collective good of the nation. As a result, today we can see all these diverse cultures, religions, languages and life-styles conglomerated into a single Nepali nationality. All these have an environment conducive to their development in unity with others. The Rajbanshi's are one of many such peoples who have their own language, culture and the way of life.

The Rajbanshi's are the indigeneous people residing in the eastern Terai, specifically in Jhapa district. They also reside in Morang in a few number. Physically they are analogous to both the Aryans and non-Aryans. But they are closer to the Tharus and similar local inhabitants in their cultural practices and physical structures than others. They have their own unique identity and tradition. The Rajbanshi's are one of the few indigenous people in Jhapa who are somewhat suspicious and introvert. They take time to intermingle with outsiders and accept changes though they seem eager to adopt new ideas and practices.

Though Rajbanshi's are indigenous people of Nepal, they seem to be almost aside of national mainstream even in the present times due to their own narrow social values. It is yet unclear from where and when the Rajbanshi's came to the place. Similarly, from which source they originated is not clear.

Though there prevail various sayings, no scholars have yet been able to confirm there position. Scholars Hamilton and Hudson put that the Rajbanshi's and Koch's are the same. Dalton puts that they belong to the Bhuiya family. Similarly, Beharly holds that the Rajbanshi's and Paliya belong to the same race. What is certain, however, is that this group is under the influence of the Sanskrit civilisation.

The population of the Rajbanshi's inhabiting the area between the Koshi and Mechi rivers was 59,383 according to the census of 2038 BS (calculated on the basis of the Rajbanshi's speaking population). Following the 2048 census report, the number has increased to 75,360 (0.4).

The Rajbanshi language is somewhat close to a dialect of the Bengali language. This is a matrilineal community where women position is respected. Women do almost all types of works.

To see the cultural part, the Rajbanshi marriage practice is quite interesting. The groom should pay some amount to the bride-family for marriage, the amount is called "Chumana." The amount varies according to the family status and the nature and beauty of the bride. Anyone who fails to deposit "Chumana" should stay and work at the bride's residence until the amount is paid off. The Rajbanshi's also allow widow-marriage.

The Rajbanshi's are Hindus who worship various Hindu gods and goddesses. In each village they have constructed a hut as a Kali temple. They believe in supernatural spirits, magic and sorcery. They, therefore, also worship human skulls. This community worships different gods for different purposes, such as Bistothakur for water, Barmathakur for fire and so on. Dolsiruwa, Dolpawani, Maidekheli-tistabudhi, Siruwa Pawani, Bisawa Siruwa, Ranga Siruwa, Asari-Dhasari, Dadhikad, Lakkhi-puja, Anatadora etc. are some of their major festivals.

The Rajbanshi's are mainly agricultural workers who work in the fields and rear livestock. Some of them are also involved in small business. Their secondary income sources include some employment in formal establishments, cloth weaving and so on. Culturally, the Rajbanshi's are thus very rich.

Many studies have been made on other communities such as the Newars, Rais, Gurungs, Tharus, Dhimals, Chepangs, etc. in Nepal. Their culture and traditions have been preserved in written archives. But no attention has been made towards recording the culture of Rajbanshi's which is quite necessary. They failed to record their traditional and cultural richness and vivacity in time, there is a danger that the influence of 20th century modernity may erode this away.

This book through 9 headings seeks to explain the cultural, religious and traditional practices and other rituals, of the Rajbanshi's. This book is based on the published books and articles, limited though they are, by various scholars. This also records the impression of personal visits and outcomes gained through numerous discussions with elderly Rajbanshi's. I therefore, do not claim that the book is solely my creation. Any write-ups and a community's culture, tradition, art, language etc. do not amount to a person's creation. They themselves are the product of the people who belong to the community. I am, therefore, indebted to all those scholars and senior citizens because of whom the book has come to this form.

The book explains why the Rajbanshi's choose the Jhapa district and under what geographical and historical background they came in here. Why they choose this place as their place of residence, why they practice various cultures and religions and why they adopt a traditional vivacity and how it is explained in the book? This book also attempts to explain their social, traditional and religious dramas, and their folklore.

In connection with the preparation of this book, I am firstly indebted to my friend Chintamani Dhalal and elder brother literatueur Bhawani Ghimire who inspired and assisted me to help produce this book. Ten years ago, he accompanied me to various Rajbanshi dwellings in Jhapa, especially at Ghailadubba. He also explained me whatever he had known about the Rajbanshi's.

The book was prepared in the Nepali language. My friend

Yog Raj Bhattarai assisted me in translating it into English. I owe my debts to him for his assistance, and it was really a tedious task without which the book would not have been possible. The assistance of my respected Guru Krishna Bahadur Udaya (Trichandra Campus) has always been a source of inspiration to me. I would like to note the appreciation of my friends Yagyanath Acharya, Bimal Sharma (Trichandra Campus), Mukunda Kattel (INSEC), my childhood friend Madan Tuladhar (Thamel) and other friends Madhuman Pradhan, Bishwambhar Lal Pradhan, Lekhnath Bhandari, Raghu Lamichhane, Nara Nath Luitel, Krishna Murari Adhikari (Ombahal), Shree Ram Shrestha (Machhendrabahal) for their assistance and inspiration.

My spouse Ila Gautam, sons Shovendra Gautam and Nissim Gautam have also helped me in various ways. Similarly, the Rajbanshi's of Jhapa have overtly and covertly assisted me. I am sorry for my failure to list so many names which I could not due to the reason of space, specially the Rajbanshi friends and seniors.

Thamel,
June, 2004

Dr. Rajesh Gautam

Contents

Preface 5

1 **Introduction:** **15**
- — Geographical and Historical Background of Jhapa District / 15
- — Introduction of Rajbanshi's / 24
- — Origin of Rajbanshi's / 32
- — Caste and Clan of Rajbanshi's / 33
- — The Importance of Rajbanshi's with reference to Nepal / 34

2 **Rajbanshi Society** **37**
- — Settlements / 37
- — Family / 40
- — Relationships (Kith and Kin) / 43
- — Social Relation / 46
- — Dresses / 47
- — Ornaments / 48
- — Food (Victuals) / 49
- — Pots and Instruments / 50
- — Weapons / 50
- — Status of Male and Female in Rajbanshi Society / 51
- — The Chumana System / 52

— The Danguwa System (Widow Marriage) / 53

3 Rajbanshi Life-cycle and Rituals **55**

(*a*) Birth Sacrament / 56
(*b*) Khirchhuwa / 59
(*c*) Karnachhed / 60
(*d*) Marriage Custom / 62
— Suba Dekha / 63
— Dulha Tilkhibar / 64
— Pan Katani / 64
— Dahanguwa (Dalikhara) / 65
— Sandos / 66
— Karali Bhar / 66
— Adibas / 67
— Baerati (Chapahari) / 68
— Bhar Bhat / 72
— Basya Baiha / 73
— Ghar Bas / 74
— Athubari / 74
— Sagani Mangana / 75
— Madar Katani / 75
— Shesh Bidagi / 75
— Various Kinds of Marriages / 76
(*e*) Death Rites / 76

4 Economic Status (Rajbanshi Economy): **84**

(*a*) Economic Resources (Income Sources) / 86
(*i*) Agriculture / 86
(*ii*) Trade (Business) / 88
(*iii*) Cattle Fostering / 88
(*iv*) Labour / 89
(*v*) Supplementary Income Sources / 90
(*b*) Expenditure / 91

5 Festival **94**

(*a*) Pawani / 94
(*i*) Dol-Siruwa / 94
(*ii*) Dol-Pawani / 95

(iii) Bedekhaili Tistabudhi / 96
(iv) Siruwa Pawani / 97
(v) Bisawa Siruwa / 100
(vi) Ranga Siruwa / 100
(vii) Kad Siruwa / 101
(viii) Asari Ghasari 101
(ix) Dadhi-Kad / 102
(x) Jatra / 102
(xi) Lakhi Puja / 103
(xii) Bhaktiyar System / 105
(xiii) Jituwa Pawani / 108
(xiv) Ananta Dora / 109

6 Religious Beliefs: **112**
(i) God and Goddesses of Houses / 114
(ii) God and Goddesses of the Village / 114
(iii) Ghosts / 115

7 Songs, Dances and Dramas: **121**
(a) Songs and dances / 121
(b) Dramas / 122
(i) Social and Traditional Drama / 123
(ii) Religious drama / 124
(iii) Folk Songs of Rajbanshi's / 124
(c) Language / 129

8 Educational Status **132**

9 Conclusion **135**
Cultural Aspecct / 137
Social Point / 138

Bibliography **141**

Pictorials **145**

I

Introduction

Geographical and Historical Background of Jhapa District

On the map of the world, Nepal is located in the middle of the latitude 26° to 30° and longitude 80° to 88°, having the length of 550 miles and an area of 56,000 square miles. Mostly, northern part of Nepal is covered with snowy mountains. According to the administrative and political divisions, Nepal is divided into 14 zones and 75 districts. Among them Mechi Zone is situated in the far eastern part of Nepal. Mechi Zone is divided into 4 developmental districts; which are: Taplejung, Panchthar, Ilam and Jhapa. The three districts are mountainous except Jhapa. Jhapa is fully in Terai region. It is better to mention the brief historical background of Jhapa before mentioning its geographical background.

Present area of Jhapa district was included in the broad area of Morang region before the kingdom of Nepal being united. The King of Morang region was Vijaya Narayan while Rudra Sen and lateron Mukunda Sen I of Sen dynasty were ruling in Palpa. The Palpali Sen dynasty had got much more colonies in the eastern part of Palpa, so the King of Palpali

Sen dynasty sent help for the purpose of helping King Ratna Malla of Kathmandu Valley.[1]

Lohang Sen, the youngest son of Mukunda Sen I (1518-1553 A.D.) defeated the small Thakurai's upto Koshi river and included this area in his own kingdom in reference to the victory of eastern Terai. But the Morang region; across the Koshi, where there was Bijayapur Kingdom, was not easy to win. In the meantime, there was an opinion contrast between King Bijaya Narayan and his Kirant ministers. But at the same time, because of the death of Bijaya Narayan, that region was easily been handled by Lohang Sen and the post of ministers were given to the Kirants according to the commitment made earlier. It continued lateron too. The state boundary of Mukunda Sen I had spread near to Sarhad of present Nepal. But Mukunda Sen divided his vast state in small pieces and distributed them to his descendants. According to this division, Lohang Sen, the winner of Koshi zone, became the King of this region. After his death, his sons Rajab Sen and Harihar Sen became the kings respectively, but on the turn of Harihar Sen, his state was divided into two pieces because of the clash between the sons of his two queens about their ancestors' state. After giving the region west to Koshi to his youngest son Shuva Sen and east of Koshi to his late son Chhatrapati's infant son Indu Bidhana Sen, he died. At that time, the border of Bijayapur Thakurai was spread from Koshi to Testa. Lohang Sen's family ruled this area until Prithvi Narayan Shah merged it in his Kingdom. Prithivi Narayan Shah was getting victory towards east forward in the context of uniting Nepal. At the same time in 1973 B.S., two company armies attacked and captured the Chaudandi in the leadership of Bakshi Aviman Singh Basnet and Sardar Parathi Bhandari. Earlier, the king of that place, Karna Sen had already ran away towards Bijayapur[2].

---

1. Bal Chandra Sharma, *Nepal Ko Aitihasik Rup Rekha*. Fourth Edition (Baranasi: Krishna Kumari Devi, 2023, B.S., p. 201).
2. Baburam Acharya, *Shree 5 Badamaharajadhiraja Prithvinarayan*, 1st edition, (Kathmandu Press Secretariat of His Majesty The King, 2024, p. 62).

After this, Prithvi Narayan Shah started preparations to attack Bijayapur. Prithvi Narayan Shah had already made friendship with Warren Hastings, British Governor of India at that time, writing letters on 27th May 1973 and 14th January, 1974 Bikrami because of the doubt that Buddhi Karna Rai; the all-in-all minister of that place before in case of attack, will be helped by English forces. Suddenly, Aviman Singh Basnet attacked Bijayapur in the mid-time of rainy season making his armies cross the Koshi river riding on elephants. King Karna Sen had already gone to Purniya with his family and Buddhi Karna Rai escaped by riding on elephant. Gorkhali conquered Bijayapur on 17th July, 1974 (Bikrami). Then the armies commanded by Aviman Singh captured Sangurigadhi immediately and thus made an entrance to the hilly areas. The armies commanded by Aviman Singh Basnet moved forward to get victory had captured upto Tibet border in north of next Kirant and upto the river Tamor to the east. At this time, all the region ruled by Limbus became converted under the ownership of Gorkhali's because of being situated at the west of watering level of the hill Singlia and being agreed to be sheltered under Gorkhali's by the Limbus who were being disturbed by Sikkim. In this way, the border of Nepal was spread to Singlila at the hill and upto the Kankai river at the plain.[3]

According to Baburam Acharya, there was a clash between Kamadatta Sen and his minister Buddhi Karna Rai about the region upto Tista; east to Kankai river. Consequently, Buddhi Karna Rai ran away towards Purniya and settled there. Then he got murdered Kamadatta Sen using the trick of the armies in his favour in Bijayapur. On the other side, grabbing the opportunity of the clash between the king and his minister, Nangyal-Fun Chou, the King of Sikkim, had included the area of Ilam ruled by Bijayapur state in his own kingdom.[4] Also in Terai, the region east to Kankai river, had already been captured by Sikkim.

---

3. Ibid, p. 609-12.
4. Ibid, p. 603.

In the socio-political state of that time if Sikkim had been attacked, China also might have clashed in the care of Pancham Lama and Dalai Lama as well as English people being possible enemies. While getting a plea, Prithvi Narayan Shah was not in a hurry to attack Sikkim. But while getting the area of Limbus ruled under Gorkhali's, the King of Sikkim sent his own young son Diwan accompanied by Aviman Singh Basnet to the Gorkhali's for the purpose of establishing relationship with them by the medium of negotiation. Aviman Singh also sent a message to the King of Sikkim in which he stated that Sikkim will be preserved if Ilam, captured by Sikkim from the King of Bijayapur and the area upto Tista is returned. According to these negotiations the King of Sikkim signed an agreement made and stamped on 25th of September. As a result, Aviman Singh Basnet broadened the border of Nepal upto Tista which was out of the ruling area of English people.[5] After that, this area had been owned by the Nepal State for many years. Nepal was attacked from around 1814 A.D. taking plea to the authority of Syuraj of western Nepal and the area of Butawal. According to one of the English writer the castle of Nepalese army was in Bijayapur in this region. Under the commandership of Major Letter, Company armies attacked and captured Ghampur which is between Biratnagar and Rangeli as well as Jhapa Market.

In the beginning of the war, company armies had got many troubles (whips) although the result of the war was not in favour of Nepal. Consequently, Treaty of Sugauli was signed on 28th November, 1815. According to this treaty, the terrain region from Mechi to Tista was handed over to the authority of East India Company. The river Mechi, became the eastern international border of Nepal since that day.

Jhapa had been declared as the region of Morang until the present administrative and political division took place. Only after the present administrative and political division,

---

5. John Pemble, *The Invasion of Nepal*, Ford, Clerendn Press 1971, p. 245.

it has been standing as a distinct district. According to the geographical condition, Jhapa district is located between 26.20° northern latitude to 26.50° and 87.39° eastern longitude to 88.12°.

Ilam is the northern border of this district. Similarly, Ratuwa river has separated this district from Morang district in the west and Mechi river and pillars of Dasa Gaja has separated it from the state of West Bengal in India and Bihar region respectively. This district seems rectangular sized, of which east to west is long and north to south is wide. The length of this district from east to west is about 46 kms and width from north to south is 29 kms. The total area of this district is 1532 kms and according to the National Census held in 2028 B.S., its population was 2,47,698. Is it not a wonderful thing that Indian culture, language and caste affects Jhapa directly or indirectly because of being touched by the both borders of it.

The climate of Jhapa district is mostly hot because of being in the height of 125 to 200 meters from the level of the sea. This place is not so healthy because it is too hot in summer and the climate of winter season lacks hotness. It is difficult to measure the proper temperature of this district due to lack of centre for weather observation within this district, but according to the tabled information taken at Biratnagar airport of Morang district, touching this district, the average maximum temperatue goes upto 30.6° centigrade (87°F) in summer and minimum 14.2° centigrade (57.50°F) in winter.

There are many places for sight-seeing especially the ancient historical residues in Jhapa. But there has not been any scientific as well as ordinary research about these historical facts and residues uptill now. Satasidham, Birat Pokhar, Kilagadh, Lukali, Kichakbadh, Susamayagadh, etc. are the main historical places of Jhapa district. According to the customary assertions, their brief details are given respectively as following :

(a) ***Satasidham:*** This Dham is situated in the lap of Chulachuli hill which is in the far-northern Jhapa. It is shaped like the udder of the cow and similarly many stones in the shape of various Gods and Godesses are available here. Also big bricks are found here. According to customary assertions, all of these are the ruins of the palace of King Birat.

(b) ***Birat Pokhar:*** There are big ponds near the rent free land, Anarmani. According to assertions, these ponds had been made by King Birat and among them, the queen of King Birat had used a pond to have a bath daily.

(c) ***Killagadh:*** The Gadh is situated at about one mile from Anptari. There are some of the old ruins and ponds found near it. People of this place say that the gadh is of the Mahabharat time.

(d) ***Lukali:*** This place is a little far from Shanischare. According to the oldest inhabitants of this place, Royal prince Duryodhan had made a carrying off of cows from the den of King Birat and had hidden them at this place.

(e) ***Kichakbadh:*** In the south of Bhadrapur, there is a place named Kichakbadh. Here is a Gadh and a pond. According to the assertions, here was a theatre of King Birat and it is the same place where Bhimsen killed Kichak while trying to rape Draupadi. A fair takes place every year at this place in winter. Mainly, Rajbanshi's use to reach there to take part in it. After having a bathe and chasity, they use to offer their offerings to their father and fore-fathers and desire the welfare of their ancestors, being more generous in honour of deceased ancestors. Here are found big bricks, hard round objects of clay and coins.

(f) ***Susamayagadh:*** This Gadh is situated on the eastern side of Gauriganj market of Jhapa. Now-a-days, it is fully covered by bushes. This Gadh seems very big. According to the traditional concept, the construction of this Gadh had been done by Trigartaraj Susharma. The river Kishni has been flowing near Susamaya Gadh. It is stated in Mahabharat that Trigartaraj Susharma had passed a whole night on the bank of

Kishni (Krishna) river after attacking and making prisoner to King Birat. According to the customary assertions, existing Kishni river is the Krishna river of that time.

Upto 2007 B.S., no other castes were able to settle down in this place except Dhimal, Rajbanshi, Tharu, Meche, Satar, Bantar and Jhangar and they might have severely suffered from Malaria. Brahmin, Chhetri, Newar and other hilly races have entered in this region after the peoples' revolution of 2007 B.S. The number of migrants from hilly races has been growing at an increasing rate after 2017 B.S., except the inhabitants from the very beginning. Comparatively, due to continuous migration the number of migrators, became higher than the number of earliest inhabitants after the eradication of Malaria in Jhapa. In this way, hilly area has been emptying whereas the population of Jhapa has been increasing day-by-day. Consequently, the inhabitants of Jhapa from the very beginning have been disappearing whereas the problem of settlement having increased, the slogan that "The green forest, property of Nepal" is only in the position of existing in the statement. Silk cotton tree (Simal), Catechu (Khayar), Sisau, Sakhuwa and Rajbrikshsa are the trees found in the forest of this place. Similarly, among the wild animals: deers, Mithun cows, wild buffaloes, elephants, tigers, bears, leopards, ghorals and rabbits are found here. The study of this district can be done dividing it into two parts according to the nature of the land, inspite of having plain field:

(a) Low lying land area of the north.
(b) Terai area of the south.

(a) ***Low lying land area of the north:*** The area of the land from Ilam district; the northern border of the district, which is being precipitous to the south is called "Low lying land region". This region is spread between Mechi in the east to Ratuwa in the west at about the width of 12.8 Km. This region especially and fully contains sand, pebbles, stones and unsubstantial soil. The bushes and trees in this region used to be thick. That's why this region is also called the "Char Koshe Jhadi" of Nepal. As in other terain districts of this region, except the

big rivers flowing from the north, most of the rivers and streams flow under the surface of the land in this district too and appear while entering in the Terai region. Shantinagar and Bahundagi are in the highest position and northern part of this district. These places are at the height of 381 metres from the sea level. The northern part of Topgachi and Shivaganj Village Development Committee and about all the parts of Damak Municipality, Surunga, Pararbaupi, Budhabare, Shanischare, Dhaijan, Dhulabari, Shantinagar, Bahundagi, Nakalbanda etc. Village Development Committees are contained in this low lying land area.

(b) ***Terain area of the South:*** This part of the land is fully in Terain region. More than 50% land of this district is in this region. This territory of the land is most fertile because of the sandy part of clay depositied by floods of the river. The soil in this region becomes damp and soft because of the arrival of the small as well as big rivers being dried up in low lying land area in this territory. That's why this part of the land is fertile enough. The main rivers of this district flowing north to south because of the land slope being steeped north to south, used to be adjusted with the big rivers flowing from the east in India. All these rivers have been flowing to the South from Ilam district. Among these rivers, Mawa Stream, Ratuwa Stream, Kankai river, Biring River, Anduwa Stream, Deuniya Stream, Handiya Stream, Timai Stream, Ninda River, Mechi River etc. are located west to east respectively. These rivers had made this district the storehouse of edible food by providing irrigation facility, whereas thousands of acres (about 5/8 area) of the land used to be flooded by them yearly, and as a result millions of rupees are being lost.

The main crops of this place are: Paddy, wheat, jute, mustard, pulse, sugarcane and a little millet, etc. Among the main crops paddy and jute are the most. Now-a-days, the production rate of maize and millet is also equally increasing in the northern area of Jhapa.

Rajbanshi, Tharu, Satar, Dhimal, Meche, Brahmin, Chhetri, Magar, Newar, Gurung, Limbu, Kumhal, Tamang, Damai, Kami, Sarki, etc. are the main inhabitant castes of this district. Only the settlement of Thakali's found in other parts of the country is not found here. Besides a small number of

Marwadi's having the profession of business, have settled in the market areas of Shanischare, Dhulabari, Bhadrapur, Damak, Jayapur, Budhabare, etc. The population growth is in excess in this area as compared with other parts of this district. According to the census of 2038 B.S., the average number of family is 4.5 members whereas the growth rate of Jhapa is 5.6. Particularly, the number of families that have migrated here from Taplejung, Panchthar, Ilam, Terathum, Dhankuta, Assam, Sikkim of India and Bhutan, is large. The culture of the castes and also the nationalism of the inhabitants of this place from the very beginning is going to vanish because of the excessive immigration from outside. The main causes of being so, are their own innocence and lack of awareness. The progressive attitude and cleverness is more in the castes entering from outside by nature. The earlier habitants have not made progress in front of them and they haven't got any inspiration and opportunity to do so. Among all the inhabitants, from the very beginning, Rajbanshi's are ahead. The status of the castes Dhimal, Satar, Tharu and Meche, is becoming delicate day-by-day.

The main road for transport in Jhapa district is Mahendra Highway. Besides this highway among other main roads, Birtamod to Bhadrapur, tarred road from Birtamod to Shanischare and the road from Charali to Ilam in which about 90% of construction has been completed recently, are existing. Among the main gravelling roads inside the district are—Kankarvitta to Bahundangi, Bhadrapur to Kechana and Damak to Gauradaha linked with Gauriganj. Bus services on these gravelling roads is available in winter season only but all the traffic used to be stopped in rainy season.

Similarly, in some of the main places of Jhapa, telephone; the medium of communication and also electricity has been managed. Attempts on providing these facilities more pervasively at all the places of the district, are being made. From the Kankai river of this district, the work of irrigation and electricty generation is being done under a large project. After the completion of it, drastic changes can be expected in economic and social development of this district.

Rajbanshi's (Indigenous People)
An introduction:

Inspite of Rajbanshi's being seen at a glance can be compared with Aryans in physical structure, characteristics equal to the shape and colour of Anaryas can also be seen in their physical structure. Rajbanshi's who have been settling in Jhapa are having a distinguished caste having their own existence and Fundamental lineal succession, have equity in many ways with Tharus and similar local castes in customs and physical structure, but they don't belong to the Hindu Caste hierarchy. According to the classification of people, made on the basis of mother tongue by the census of 2028 B.S.; The number of Rajbanshi language speakers is 41,244 which is the largest number next to the speakers of Nepali languages (1,10,797)[5]. These people are also in Morang district in a mentionable number (13,739)[6].

From the very beginning Rajbanshi's settled in Jhapa are the indigenous people having their own ethics and who have narrow tendency in their character and they are unable to adjust soon with unfamiliar beings; always doubtful to them. Also they don't have the courage to accept the changes inspite of being curious towards new things and affairs. Inspite of being settled from the very beginning in Nepal, it is felt that they are separated from the complete national flow in the present state too, because of their own narrow social norms and values. Rajbanshi's who don't want to settle with other communities except their own, are from where and when they came to settle here and to which original family they belong to has not been ascertanied yet.

Many of the scholars have different opinions about it. Some interesting customary assertions, prevailing in Rajbanshi's community themselves, say that they are the Chhetries of Surya Dynasty and of 'Kashyap' clan. This is the matter of Silver age that one day Kirtaviryarjun, the King of

---

5. Swayambhu Lal Shrestha, *Hami Nepali*, 1st Edition, Lalitpur: Shretha Prakashan, 2028, p. 69.
6. Ibid.

Rajbanshi's had gone to the forest with his army for hunting. But it was the surprise on that day they couldn't hunt wild animals. It became evening while hunting and the King had no time to return back to his palace, crossing the thick forest. Thus, all of them together with the King stayed at one place of the forest. The King was in the state of solitariness because of being hungry and thirsty. The King sent some of his soldiers in search of water and food. At a distance, the soldiers who were in search of food, saw a hermitage. The hermitage had been owned by the Seer Janmadagni; father of Parshuram. The Seer was in his hermitage. The Seer and the soldiers of the King introduced each other. The soldiers narrated to the Seer about the present condition of the King not being able to find anything.

The Seer said to the soldiers, "Go and convey this message to the King that I will serve them with warm hospitality tonight". After that, the King, his aristocrats, courtiers and the soldiers came to Seer's ashram and they were accomodated in proper places. Janmadagni welcomed them providing all kinds of food in the golden and silver made dishes and cups according to their post and honour. The taste of food was supernatural. This was a supicious matter to the King that from where this Seer in his small hermitage, having religious penance, brought so much valuable sweets and food as well as the cups and dishes made of Gold and Silver. The King became too curious and ordered his spies to find out the mystery. The spies started to inspect all around the cottage. After seeing the cow "Kamdhenu" of the religious sage which was the gift of Indra; the emperor of the heaven, all the mystery was solved. The King asked for the cow—'Kamdhenu' promising to give thousands of cows instead, but the Seer refused. The King ordered his soldiers to carry the cow forcefully untieing it. Because the Seer was not in favour of loosing the cow Kamdhenu in any conditions, there was a wrestling between the King and the Seer and at that time force was used. Alone Seer, couldn't defeat the King. The king killed the religious Sage and returned to his palace carrying the cow. On the other side, Parshuram, being too much angry, moved here and there holding an axe in his hand telling all of the Chhetries to be killed because by the force of his religious penance he had come to know all the doings of the King. Parshuram defeated the King and killed him. The apprehension of danger created by Parshuram hang all over the villages. All the residents of that state and nereby villages ran away from their houses because of the thought of not being saved from the dangerous attitude of Parshuram. Parshuram had put his sacred cord off in order to not being recognized as a Chhetri. Some of the people hanged garlic and onions around their houses. Till that time, no Brahmins and Chhetries had used garlic and onion. The use of garlic and onion had been done by Vaishyas and Shudras only. In some festivals uptill now the tradition of hanging the garlic and onion is seen in the houses of Rajbanshi's. In this way, because of being afraid of Parshuram all the living beings escaped hither and thither. Some of them arrived at Bihar, Bengal and Assam of present India as well as Jhapa and Morang of Nepal. According to further story, the Brahmins had gradually been stopped to work as priests, because of the hostility made with Parshuram and they used to do the acts of religious rites themselves. But now-a-days Brahmins are less used as priests in the acts of religious rites because of not being able to break the tradition atonce. There is another customary assertion about it. According to the prevailing assertion, present Rajbanshi's are from the dynasty of Kichak; the commander-in-chief or the brother-in-law of King Birat mentioned in Mahabharat. Kichak had been killed by Bhimsen while trying to rape Draupadi. The place of Kichakbadh is situated at a little distance from Bhadrapur.

Rajbanshi's have been living in between Koshi and Mechi rivers. They are found in great number towards India too. Mainly they have settled in Bihar, Bengal and Assam provinces in India. There are some of the Newars having Rajbanshi tribe. Approximately, there is no any similarity between Newar Rajbanshi's and the Rajbanshi's of Jhapa. These Newar Rajbanshi's use to say that theirs is no any kind of relationship and equality with the Rajbanshi's of Jhapa. We have found some of the records[7] that prove the marriage of King Pratap Malla of Kathmandu with Rupmati, the daughter of Bir Narayan who was the king of Koch Bihar. Consequently, it is obvious that Mallas and Koch (Rajbanshi's) were equal in their tribes and castes. Probably, the Rajbanshi race, found in Newar community, might have come in Kathmandu as a result of marital relation established at that time. In this way, it seems that there is a harmonious relationship between the Koch (Rajbanshi's) and Malla kings. Leaving these matters as present questions, there are some of the opinions stated here from different scholars about Rajbanshi's; "from where and when, as well as to which dynasty source they belong?"

An English writer named Hamilton has written about the presence of this caste at this place in 1802 and 1803 A.D. He has stated that these Koch's or Rajbanshi's, speaking a kind of Bengali language in the eastern part of Bijayapur state, are the main inhabitants from the very beginning of Kamrup.[8]

Hudson has declared that the area of Koch's is spread between the Dhanashree river in the east and Kankai river in the west which is located in the middle of the latitude 80° to 93.5° east and 25° to 27° north longitude.[9] According to this fact, it is clear that Koch's inside the border of present Nepal, are in a small number of the total population of Koch's in this area. Hamilton and Hudson have even presented their own different data about the population of them at that time. According to the statement given by Hamilton, at about 3.5 million on 1802 to 1803 A.D. and approximately 8 million was the number of them including the Koch's who eclipsed the Islam religion according to Hudson.[10]

---

7. Gautambajra, Royal Palace Hanuman Dhoka, Kathmandu: Institute of Nepal and Asia, T.U. 2033) Appendix 16, p. 203.
8. Francis Buchanan Hamilton, *An Account of the Kingdom of Nepal*, New Delhi, Manjusri Publishing House, 1971, pp. 119, 125, 156.
9. Brain Hodgson, *Miscellaneous Essays Relating to Indian Subject*, Vol. 1, London Trubnerco, Ludgate Hill 1880, pp. 107-119.
10. Ibid, pp. 107-119.

The exact number of them has not been known yet. It is clear that the main places of their residence outside the political border of Nepal are Sikkim, Bhutan and India, because of being assumed as less than one million including other castes called Koch and the Rajbanshi's of Jhapa and Morang district of Nepal.

In Tabakat Nasiri, which had been edited on 1918 B.S., Koche, Meche and Tharus have come and settled in 'Kamrup'. According to Hudson, Koch's had come from Aryans. In his opinion, Haju established the state of Koch's. Afterwards, Bishu; a grandson of Haju being Hindu and named as Bishwa Singh ruled it. Later on, it is stated that they were known as Rajbanshi's instead of telling Koch to themselves.[11]

Dalton had told them "Anarya" because of the appearances of Koch's and also he had stated that they (Koch's) were from Dravid lineage and Bhuiyan family.[12]

Weaverly has assumed that Koch, Rajbanshi and Palia are from the same caste.[13]

There is an interesting historical tradition about the co-relation between the cultural groups named Rajbanshi's who are directly impressed from Sanskrit civilization and the Koch's or so-called Meches who have their own distinct characteristics and are not impressed by others.[14] According to the customary assertions, first of all there were only Koch races and in this territory of Nepal and India, there was a powerful state of Koch's which was established by Haju. Bishu, the grandson of Haju was brave. He defeated the neighbouring petty rulers and made a beautiful city named 'Koch Bihar' which place is still found in India.

Having seen the bravity of Bishu, Brahmins catagorized the ruler of Koch in Chhetri group and gave an honour named Chhetri caste indicating Rajbanshi, based on Sanskrit instead

11. Journal of Asiatic Society of Bengal, Vol. XVIII, Part II (1849), pp. 704-706.
12. Descriptive Ethnology of Bengal (1872), pp. 80-92.
13. Census Report of Bengal, Vol. I (1872), p. 130.
14. Dor Bahadur Bista *"People of Nepal"* 2nd ed., Kathmandu, Ratna Pustak Bhandar, 1972, pp. 134-37.

of Koch. These Koch's became Rajbanshi since that very time. Bishu, himself became King Bishwa Singh. Most of the poor Koch's became Moslems. But some of the Koch's didn't change their religion and followed their traditional religious beliefs. In these days too, they are popular by the name of Koch. They use to speak Koch language. But Rajbanshi's use to speak a kind of speech (language) similar to the Bengali language which is called the speech of Rajbanshi's. There is some effect of Bengali language but there is a mixture of Assamese language in the speech of the Rajbanshi's of Assam.[15]

According to Doctor Hunter, Bishwa Singh; the grand son of Haju became initiated in Hindu religion and has changed from Koch to Rajbanshi. Superiors and farmers were called Rajbanshi's but the labourers getting wage remained Koch's as such.[16] N.B. Rauni has stated that they had left their own old habits after marital relation being established with Koch's and Hindus. They are mostly alike with Bengali's.[17]

According to H. Boilyu, Koch's or Rajbanshi's were not Hindus from the very beginning but the inhabitants changed their religion to Hindu later. The kings of Jalpaiguri and Koch Bihar are from the same dynasty but the kings of Jalpaiguri claim themselves as belonging to the families of Shiva and Yogini Devi. They used to say themsevles as from Shiva dynasty. Thus, Koch's used to say themselves as belonging to the dynasty of the King or Rajbanshi. Now-a-days, some of the Rajbanshi's use to say themselves as belonging to the dynasty of Chhetries who had escaped while at the destruction of Chhetries by Parshuram.[18]

Getal has stated that Koch's and Rajbanshi's are separate castes. Koch's used to say Rajbanshi to themselves but Koch's

15. Swayambhu Lal Shrestha, "*Hami Nepali*" 1st Edition, Lalitpur: Shrestha Prakashan, 2028 B.S. pp. 69-70.
16. Statistical Account of Bengal (1876), Vol. I, extracted by Swayambhu Lal Shrestha, "*Hamro Garima*" 1st Edition, Bhadrapur, Alok Prakashan, 2032 B.S., p. 66.
17. Wild Tribes of India (1882), p. 146.
18. Census Report of The District of Jalpaiguri, 1891, extracted by Swayambhu Lal Shrestha, *"Hamro Garima"*, p. 67.

are Mangolians and Rajbanshi caste is 'Dravid'. This name has been got by them before the Koch's being the King whose colour is as black as Mongolian's appearance or they are Koch mixed races.[19]

According to O. Mel, Rajbanshi's or Baruwa Mugs, Bengali woman and Barmi or Bengali male had born from mother Arakani.[20]

On the basis of the physical structure and facial colour of Rajbanshi's, Rijale has classfied them as belonging to Mangol Dravidian family and also has said that Rajbanshi, Koch and Bhumi castes speak Bengali language. But it cannot be declared that they are from the dynasty of Indian Aryans only by this linguistic reason. Their physical symbols have helped enough in comparison to their language in order to decide about them. We have no any obvious factual proof uptill now, although it is true that Rajbanshi Koch's had used to speak their castewise language before two or three generations. Once upon a time the following castes had used to be known as the well organized castes having a safe culture: Ahir, Dim, and Dushath of Bihar and other provinces of India. Similarly, Mujur, Jat, Mejo and Rajput of Rajputana and Panjab, Koli, Kahar, and Maratha of Bombay; Bangadi, Bauri Chandal, Kaibari, Rajbanshi and Kuchu of Bengal; Mal, Naiyar and Bailatla of Madras. Their social and other conditions had not been discriminated as inferior in the social legislation of Hindus.

Now-a-days, all the inhabitant castes from the very beginning or some of the communities of it have catagorised themselves as in the sequence of a new tribe under the Hindu Socio status. Although they used to assume as more ancient to their own history of their caste, but they are being separated from other socially accepted (valid) high castes by their own names and some of the special customs having by themselves, e.g. most of the Koch's from Jalpaiguri, Rangpur and Deen area used to introduce themselves as permanent Rajbanshi's and as from the side of a Mang Kshetri's generation. According

19. Census Report of Bengal, 1891.
20. Census Report of India. Vol. V, Part I, 1911.

to their customary assertions, long long ago, the Hindu Kshetries having escaped towards north-east Bengal because of the fear of Parshuram's anger, were their own ancestors. They used to call themselves as the family of Dasharath, father of Ramchandra. Their affinity is also same to the customs of Hindu religion. Besides it, they have been using to name their own lineage which is same to the Brahmins. So, they are in a great difficulty these days because they all have been claiming that they are under Kashyap clan. As a result, they have been compelled to be in opposite to the rules of Brahmins because there is no any custom and tradition to marry in the same lineage in Brahmins. This fault of them must have improved as the time passes on by the help of their own priests. At last, there is the possibility of no difference between the Indian Aryans and themselves.

India is such a country where traditional concepts and customary assertions are assumed as history and it also happens so as being compelled. As stated in the story mentioned above, some times ago the area of Koch Bihar, must have belonged to the Manga Kshetries who had come there after escaping and some powerful patriarches from higher castes have ruled over the lower caste communities and less powerful than them. This is a simple matter to be such as an event in the context of Indian history.[21]

According to the study about the different opinions of different scholars mentioned above the possibility is obvious that Rajbanshi is the name of a new caste. The greatest possibility is that they were under Koch caste before making public announcement by themselves as Rajbanshi caste. Their own public announcement about having 'Kashyap clan' proves that they have come in Brahmin or Hindu religion only after many years of naming themselves as Rajbanshi's. When they gave up their own customs and followed Brahmin or Hindu religion, they didn't know to separate their clan inspite of being in the same tribe. Consequently, they are opposite to

---

21. Sir Herbert Railey, *The People of India*, Second edition, London; W. Thacker and Co., 1915, pp. 11, 40, 74, 75, 76, 99, 120, 126.

the Hindu or Brahmin religion accepting the compelledness of being married within the same clan.

Origin of Rajbanshi

Now-a-days, we don't have any historical evidence about the origin or presence of Rajbanshi tribe in Jhapa before unifying Nepal by Prithvi Narayan Shah. After 25/30 years of joining the Bijayapur State in Nepal at about 1803 A.D. a preliminary information about the contemporary life styles of the inhabitants of Jhapa district was given by Francis Hamilton. At that time, Jhapa of those days, was governed by Bijayapur State. According to the description about the Bijayapur State, Koch or Rajbanshi tribe had been living in the east and people having Gaganai tribe as well as Maithili language in the west.[22]

In addition to the information given by Hamilton mentioned above, A. Campbell had written about the people of this area in 1839 A.D. He was one of personnel of Darjelling who had given a report to the Government of India about the Mech tribe, in which he had stated that, in this area, there was the presence of Koch (or Rajbanshi's), Dhimal, Dhawa (perhaps Tharu) and white ones.[23]

Then on 1846 A.D. a researcher and English writer named Brayen Hudson studied about Jhapa or this area. He stated in his study report that Koch, Bodo, Dhimal, Haijod, Kudi, Kebrat, Pallaha, Gaganai, Maraha etc. have settled in the 150 miles area from the Golpara of Assam to Aligunj of Morang.

It is proved that among the pertaining inhabitants of this place Rajbanshi, Dhimal, Koch's, Meche etc. tribes have settled here from ancient times according to the comparative study about the structural features between the abovementioned

---

22. Francis Buchanan Hamilton, *An Account of the Kingdom of Nepal*. New Delhi, Manjushri Publishing House, 1971, pp. 124-26.
23. A. Campbell, Notes on the Mechis, extracted from; *Mechi to Mahakali* (Part I) Kathmandu: Department of Communication, 2031 B.S.

tribes and the inhabitants of Jhapa district in those days. Although there are some of the new caste holders too. So far as the question about the origin or presence of Rajbanshi caste in Jhapa is concerned, it is clearly proved by the facts mentioned above that Rajbanshi's have settled in Jhapa after 25/30 years of the victory of this area by Prithvi Narayan Shah. Inspite of assuming the possibility of settling of them before unifying Nepal by Prithvi Narayan Shah, we cannot declare about their settlement in this area because of not having any historical evidence. But at about 1803 A.D. Francis Hamilton stated about Koch and Rajbanshi's in reference to provide information of contemporary people and life styles of them in this area. On the basis of his report, there is no any doubt that Rajbanshi's have settled in Jhapa since 1803 A.D.

The Caste and Clan of Rajbanshi's (Totems):

The Rajbanshi's of Jhapa used to claim that they are from the dynasty of Suryavanshi Kshetris having the clan 'Kashyap'. There are seven castes in this community, e.g.. (1) Rajbanshi, (2) Lakhata Rajbanshi, (3) Tajpuria, (4) Koch, (5) Ramaniya Kahal, (6) KOI Makara, (7) Bona Rajbanshi. The Rajbanshi's of Jhapa used to write 'Rajbanshi' only while mentioning their caste. On the basis of the difference between their respected Kulguru god (Kul Thakur) within the same clan and race, they used to look different. We don't find discrimination of any kind in the Rajbanshi's of Jhapa within their own Rajbanshi caste from the point of view of caste. All of them used to participate equally from their foodings, settlings to festivals as well as their different cultural activities. There is no any variation regarding touchable and untouchable caste. They don't have the practice to mention caste after their name as in other Nepali castes. Mostly they use to write 'Singh' after the names of males and 'Sari' or 'Devi' after the names of females. After mentioning Singh, Sari or Devi, all the males and females use to write 'Rajbanshi' at the end of their names instead of caste as their surname. In this way, inspite of having different castes, they have entirely united themselves as Rajbanshi's who don't accept clan and dynasty as Hindus do while at being married to each other because of having the same clan and dynasty. Their own traditionally followed 'Kul Thakurs' are the measures to separate themselves internally. According to different 'Kul Gurus' names of this study, it is found that each and every 'Kul Thakur or Kul Guru' is representing the different sub-regions of Vaishnav religion. Some of the names of their Kul Thakurs are from Vaishnav religion which we have heard although some names are never heard too. But hearing the natural tendency of the good followed with various customary assertions and stories, we can believe that they are also in the same Vaishnav religion. Regarding the study, according to the interview taken from different persons, the following are the main Kul Thakurs (Kul Devta):

1. Chetan	2. Nityananda	3. Sataguruwa
4. Nitain	5. Jhaliya	6. Adik
7. Kabi	8. Thunthunia	9. Kuwal
10. Godaghar	11. Bejuja	12. Nikananda
13. Rakananda	14. Agal Pagal etc.	

Among these Thakurs, some are assumed as more powerful and some as less powerful. According to their customs it is good to marry the girl of equally powerful or less powerful Thakur followers. There is a traditional concept that the girl from more powerful Thakur devotee family use to be more strict than others and it is also harmful to the bridegroom to marry such girls. So, there is a tradition of having a detailed inquiry about their 'Kul Thakur' before the wedding ceremony.

Inspite of the absence of discrimination regarding caste within themselves, Rajbanshi's of Jhapa don't want to establish marital relationship with other castes. In Rajbanshi community, if a girl with a boy from other caste or vice versa establishes the marital relationship, both of them will not be boycotted by the society although will not be respected. They use to be fully conscious about their such traditional concept.

Importance of Rajbanshi's with Reference to Nepal:

After Nepal being united Prithvi Narayan Shah declared that "Nepal is the garden of four castes and thirtysix hues."

This statement has been popular and equally important in modern Nepal too. There are so many castes and clans within so small a country, although in the history of Nepal uptil now, there is no any conflict between the different castes regarding their cultural, religious as well as traditional beliefs. This is the glorious characteristic of Nepalese history. There is the prosperity of brotherhood, sisterhood and parenthood for each other in all the different castes. Having such prosperous intimacy, each and every caste is free to follow their own socio-economic, cultural and religious beliefs or traditions. In reference to Nepal each and every caste has its own importance. In the same way, Rajbanshi's, the inhabitants from the very beginning, also have their own importance as other castes like Dhimal, Satar, Meche, Danuwar etc. In the present progressive context of Jhapa, if we forget or ignore their roles and contributions, there is no doubt that the history of Jhapa will certainly be incomplete, while at settling time of them, at first there was no any map and measure of present Jhapa district. There was the land covered with grass, forest and terrible animals as well as various epidemics including Malaria, Smallpox etc. We can easily imagine that there was no any facility of having safety and security at all.

Everywhere, there was the joviality and whole-hearted approval of robbers. Everywhere ignorance and uncertainty were commonly found. We can never reject these facts. Facing these complex problems in many ways, these people used to cultivate and settled over there. They made irrigated field to the dry field and loved the land much, preparing channels for irrigation. After many years in this area, Hospitals and Health posts have been established for the health and treatment of the people. There is no any facility of health and treatment except in some towns or market areas uptill now. At that time when there was no any symbol of appearance of modern Jhapa, it was called 'Kala Pani'. Excess criminals were used to be sent to the prison of Jhapa because their life span used to be shortened being the victim of Malaria. In this way, in Jhapa of that time there was a horror-stuck of the excessive wrath of Malaria and Smallpox. At that time, there were neither transport facilities nor hospitals and schools as they are available in these days. There was no any alternative way to treat the people suffering from so many diseases and epidemics except the witch-doctors and locally available herbs. So, the tools and equipments for the treatment of that time were the inhabitants (Rajbanshi, Satar, Dhimal etc.) religous treatise, spells and domestic herbs.

Rajbanshi's important contribution is also found in this area particularly in the revolution of 2007 B.S. for the achievement of democracy. In comparison to other inhabitants from the very beginning, Rajbanshi's were ahead of them regarding civilization, consciousness and cultural activities. People having entered this area only after 2007 B.S. except the inhabitants from the very beginning. In the beginning the number of entered other castes were small and no one wanted to settle there because of the fear of Malaria, Smallpox etc., terrible diseases, robbery and excessive wrath of harmful wild animals. In the overall development of this area at that time Rajbanshi's had played a vital role. Their contribution is praisable regarding the management and establishment of schools in so many places, construction of roads and in the developmental aspect of consciousness etc.

Also at the time of Nepal being ruled by Ranas (before 2007 B.S.) posts of landlords, other social leaders and directors were given to themselves. Consequently they have been serving this area honestly. After 2007 B.S. they entered into the village level (local) and district level politics in this area. Since that point of time uptill now, Rajbanshi's have been playing a main role in the politics of village level representing more than half area of Jhapa district. In the same way, because of the big group of them in village level politics, their special importance has existed. The importance of Rajbanshi community regarding politics is great in Jhapa district. Similarly, in any way, in reference to Nepal their importance is obvious in regard to social, economic and cultural activities too.

II

Rajbanshi Society

Man is a social being. It is unrealistic to imagine the man without its society. Man remains in the society from birth to death. Another meaning of man is his basic needs in his life which can be solved (fulfilled) by the society. Man can co-operate with each other in their society. Each and every country contains its own overall obvious society and the castes of each nation have their own fundamental social philosophies. According to the social philosophy people survive themselves. Regarding this fact, Rajbanshi caste, living in the Jhapa district far east of Nepal, also have its own social life-style. Rajbanshi's can be counted as fully independent caste because Rajbanshi community contains its own fundamentality in most of the things related to their lives.

Settlements:

Village and Houses: Rajbanshi's have settled in twenty Village Development Committees (VDCs) of Jhapa district. Besides this, in other VDCs of Jhapa they have settled rarely. But their settlement can particularly be counted only in 20 VDCs in the present context. They are: (1) Ghailaduwa, (2) Anarmuni, (3) Charali, (4) Dhulabari, (5) Garamuni, (6) Kankarvitta, (7) Chandragadhi, (8) Haldibari, (9) Maheshpur, (10) Chakchaki, (11) Rajgadh, (12) Gherabari, (13) Balubari,

(14) Kechana, (15) Sharanamati, (16) Shivagunj, (17) Jhapa, (18) Gauradaha, (19) Kohabara, (20) Gaurigunj.

In this way, most of the houses of Rajbanshi's, who are settled in more than half area of Jhapa, are grouped together in the same place. There are maximum 100 houses and minimum 10/12 houses in one village. Among the many houses grouped together, one family may have owned 5/6 houses too. Thus there might be many houses in the place of 5/6 families settled together. As a result, the same houses grouped together look like a big village while looking from a distance. Because of having more houses by a single family and the tendency of living in group, the villages of Rajbanshi's seems like a hive of bees. It is found that each and every village of Rajbanshi's used to be around the houses of rich families or Devniyas. Rajbanshi's use to settle near Dewniyas because Dewniyas used to own guns and weapons. That's why they feel protected from robbers, thieves and outer attacks. In addition to this they want to socially help each other settling in a group together.

In this way, while studying about the custom of settling in a group in small place, it will be better to have a look at the geography of Terai region. Not only Rajbanshi's in Terai region use to settle in a group but also people of other castes use to do so. Such a group in settlement is being protected from thieves, robbers and wild animals as well as the right higher part of the land for the sake of being saved from sinking in the rainy season which is not found everywhere. Building houses in the paddy fields willfully be in the danger of sinking in rainy season. Therefore all of them must have been compelled to settle in the same and rarely found higher land. Gradually it is found that the environment and the tendencies of them have developed in the same way. Rajbanshi's used to use locally available resources, equipments and materials while building their houses. Rajbanshi houses used to constructed using wood, bamboo, thatch and clay etc. Only Rajbanshi's who are rich and having modern thought and feelings use to own two or three staired and zinc roofed houses. Besides this, most of the Rajbanshi houses used to be made of thatch roof, jute sticks, wall around made of bamboo etc. The outer part of the wall used to be smeared with cow-dung and clay. So the house of a Rajbanshi seems like a small cottage at a glance although they always use to smear and neat as well as clean too.

There is the custom or the tradition of building houses in all the four directions in Rajbanshi community. They use to assume that it is compulsory to build houses in three directions if they are not able to build in all the four directions. Those houses are for different purposes like kitchen in one house, store in another and living as well as wedding in the next etc. Besides this, there may be an outer house in rich Rajbanshi family. After crossing the outer house people can get the main entrance of their main house. The use of outer house is particularly for the beggars, unfamiliar ones and waiting or meeting room for the familiar ones too. The lower part of the wall of the houses are covered by mud and all the wall and the floor is smeared with the mixture of clay and cowdung as well as the pillars are being decorated with soil made flowers. Such kind of decoration is rarely found in wall and ceiling too except in pillars. The compound all over the houses used to be surrounded with the wall made by bamboo and jute sticks.

In the middle of 3/4 houses there may be a wide courtyard. There may be a fire-place in the middle of the courtyard to bask in heat in winter season. Wells used to be made near their houses for water supply. In the sides of the courtyard cages are being made for duck, swan and pigeons. The shed or hovels are being made outside and near the compound of the houses. There is a small temple or a shrine of Thakur in every house of Rajbanshi's towards east-south direction. The statues of Durga and Hanuman are established near the shrine of Thakur. The shrine of Thakur is being kept in a hut. The images of Thakur are being made raising the soil from the ground and smeared them smoothly. Basils are being planted near this. Thakur is the clan god of Rajbanshi's who is being worshiped with prays by the main person of the family daily. Around their houses they use to plant the fruits like mango, betelnut, coconut, lichi, jack fruit, banana etc. They are fond of making fruit garden although they don't know the proper way of it. Over all, at a glance the village of Rajbanshi's seems pleasant and beautiful.

Families:

The main abodes or the villages of Rajbanshi community are in the Ghailaduwa VDC (village development committee) of Jhapa. Among those villages, for the purpose of this study the 21 families of Lakadi village of Ghailaduwa VDC Ward No. 4 has been taken. Most of the families were found single in course of the study in which husband, wife and some children are included. In the course of the study, there are only three families which are joint. Among the families studied there is no any family which is likely to be great.

According to the family members' number those 42 families are classified as follows:

1 to 5 member families	28
6 to 10 member families	10
More than 10 member families	4
Total	42

According to the classification of the types and number of family members in Rajbanshi caste, it has been clear that their families are being inclined towards small and single family. Generally, most of the construction of small and single families have appeared after the death of the main person of the family. In Rajbanshi family, if there are 3/4 brothers, the eldest son lives in the joint family until his younger brothers gets married. This custom goes forward and at last parents and unmarried sisters use to live with the youngest son. Rajbanshi's are in a great number as in single families. Joint families are rarely found in comparison to the single families. Large families are negligible in number. In Rajbanshi community a son uses to live separately in another house after getting married. Now-a-days, some of the Rajbanshi's having modern thoughts and feelings, use to build bigger houses than their traditional houses and provide separate room for the son and daughter-in-law, although it is rarely found. In Rajbanshi family, there are may reasons for separating the trends of increasing the single families. Among them the main reasons are as follows:

1. Married son needs separate house
2. Because of the character of newly married girl
3. Because of the thought and feeling of happy life eating and settling of a single family.
4. Because of the interest of being separated from the joint family in which there may be workers and dependents.
5. Because of the limitation of land reform system more land cannot be owned by a single family and tendency to right system also being provided on the basis of family they have been compelled to shift in the single family.
6. Because of the lack of liaison between mother-in-law and dauther-in-law as well as father and son in the family.

The reasons mentioned above, are such that we have found common in all different castes all over Nepal. Most of the separation of the families from joint family are because of such factual reasons.

In Rajbanshi community, while studying comparatively between single and joint families, it its found that joint family is being respected economically, socially and with other reasons too. In joint family everyone obeys the chief of the house. The chief person of the family always becomes conscious about the unnecessary expenditure or the negligence in the professional tasks to be done. In Rajbanshi community most of the people like single family although joint family is accounted into progressive and respected ones.

Rajbanshi society is the father pre-eminent society. The main rights use to be owned by the father and those rights use to be transferred to the eldest son after the death of his father. Sons use to have more responsibilities in obsequal rites in honour of deceased ancestor, worshipping the god, right to property and other behavioural activities. The birth of a son in a family becomes the matter of pride and happiness.

Only by seeing the active role played by women in this community, Swyambhulal Shrestha has stated that Rajbanshi caste is the mother pre-eminent caste. It can be accepted that there is the active role of women in Rajbanshi husbandman, although no symptoms of mother pre-eminent family can be found in it. It might be that in ancient times this society may have become mother pre-eminent because of the presence of the remainings in the active role of women today. But in the present context the father or male pre-eminent society is the first characteristic among their caste's characteristics.

Both the sons and daughters are equally being cared by the parents providing proper love and nutritive food to them. There is no any difference between the son and the daughter in treating and taking care of them. They use to take care, provide good service, proper love, guidance and nutritive food to their family (children) as much as they can, although it is difficult to the Rajbanshi's to bring up their children because of many problems. The main causes of being so are as following:

(a) Because of being backward caste Rajbanshi's cannot think about their own children's bright future.
(b) Lack of proper environment to the children to be grown up.
(c) Poor economic condition.
(d) Lack of awareness and education.

Among the reasons mentioned above most common and important cause is innocence of them. They are still following their traditional concepts. They don't have the dream of planned and healthy family. There is the excess death rate of infants in the Rajbanshi society because of the lack of taking care, providing proper love, guidance, service and nutritive food to them. Also they are not being able to provide good and proper service of neatness and cleanliness as well as good health to their children. While on being suffered by various diseases, they don't consult the doctor except their witch doctors. Consequently, thousands of children are losing their life prematurely.

Relationships (kith and kin ties)

As in other societies, Rajbanshi's also divide their kith and kins (relatives) in two categories: *(a)* Blood relation, and *(b)* Marital relation.

(a) Blood relation:

In blood relation father, elder and younger brothers of father (uncles), son, grandson, elder and younger brothers etc. of the same dynasty are being categorised.

(b) Marital relation:

Daughter-in-law, daughter, son-in-law, nephews, uncle (brother of mother), brother-in-law, sister-in-law, maternal aunt, mother-in-law, father-in-law etc. are categorised in this type of relation.

In Rajbanshi society blood relatives are being greeted as 'Gathiyars' and marital relatives as 'Kutumba'. While noting, commenting or explaining about their own dynasty, Rajbanshi's use to determine or fix their kith and kins from the side of their male ancestors but not from the side of female forerunners. In other words, they use to establish their names and relations as the members of their families themselves in the background of their fathers, grandfathers and fore-fathers but not as the members of the family counted from their mothers, grandmothers and fore-mothers in which circumstances such kind of family organisation may have been presented as the family organization based on maternal relations.

Importance is being given to the blood relation or 'Guthiyar' relation than to the relation of 'Kutumba' or marital relation. It is assumed that the relation of Guthiyar is deeper and nearer (close) than marital relation. In this sense, uncle (brother of the father) is nearer than maternal uncle. Most of the words used while greeting the relatives cope with Bengali and Hindi native speakers. Besides there are some of the original greeting words for their relatives of their own but they are only occassionally used. They use respectable words like 'Tamha' ('You' while respecting) to their kith and kins, family and familiar ones as well as respectable persons. They use to greet using the word 'Tuhi' ('You' with colleagues) to their colleagues and intimate friends. They use the word 'Tor' while greeting their smaller ones on the basis of age and relation. The words, representing the relationship used as the greeting words by them, mostly cope with the relations which are familiar in Bengali and Hindi language users. For example: Sajhilka (third eldest son), Chhataka (youngest daughter), 'Ba' or 'Bap' (Father), Kaka (Father's younger brother).

Ai (Mother)
Dada (elder brother)
Bhai (younger brother)
Nandan (younger sister- in-law)
Pisai (father's sister)
'Bai' or 'Didi (elder sister)
Bahanu (Husband of elder sister)
Bhauji (wife of elder brother)
Anu (elder brother-in-law)
Pisa (father's sister's husband)
Dado (grandfather from the side of father)
Jawain (son-in-law)
Sashree (Mother-in-law)
Nandeshi (elder sister-in-law)
Mama (maternal uncle)
Dadi (grandmother or father's mother)
Bhagina (Nephew)
Susur (father-in-law)
Sali (Sister-in-law)
Mami (Wife of maternal uncle)
Nani (Grandmother from the side of mother)
Sala (Brother-in-law)

Majhilka (second eldest son)
Saghilka (third eldest son)
Chhataka (youngest daughter)
Ba or Bap (father)
Kaka (Father's younger brother)
Nana (Maternal grandfather)
Kajhilka (fourth eldest son)
Jetho (Bride, bud)

In addition to these words, Rajbanshi's have their own ideally and lovingly used words representing the relations with their neighbours and already familiar persons. Such words are also used by other civilized castes too. Except some of the greeting words, most of the words are commonly used. In Rajbanshi society, among the different relations, friendship is also an important relation. The relation of firendship has been made mainly in 3 ways. If the name of two persons is the same and if they are co-operative to each other, they use to establish the relation of friendship in their community. They use to greet as 'Mita' to each other who have established the friendship relations in such circumstances.

On the first day of the boy's wedding, specially in the night two people exchange their goods each other formally and use to be in the same boat of friendship. This sort of friendly relation is called 'Mistar'. It is compulsory to establish the relation of 'Mistar' in every boy's wedding of Rajbanshi family with same aged colleagues. The 'Mistar' is assumed as the greatest or most reliable witness. In sacred places like in temples, formal friendship is being established exchanging their things with each other which is called 'Mit'. A Mit is prohibited to look at the face of the wife of his Mit and in such a relation there are more formalities to be obeyed. Thus the relationship of 'Mistar and Mita' is being equally compared to the formal friend (Mita) of that house and rest of the two friendly related ones Mita or Mistar are also accounted as equal to Mit'. Except this, in Rajbanshi family and community, adopted father and sons also play a main role in adding relations. When a Rajbanshi feels himself helpless socially, economically and in other ways, at that time he offers betel and nut to his respectable villager for the sake of getting help (as the help from his father). Consequently he (the betelnut offerer) becomes the adopted son of the offered villager. Their relation becomes as father and son according to their needs. Now-a-days it is found that some of the Rajbanshi's are asking for help formally offering betelnut also to other castes migrated formally from the hilly areas.

In the kith and kins and as well as dynasty of Rajbanshi community, there is the tradition of respecting elders. They use to salute respectfully to their relatives and other respectable persons. Persons to be respected respectfully, they may either be male or female, should be saltued holding their legs and bending to them. There is a strange custom of respecting the respectable persons who visit their houses i.e. cleansing the respectable person's feet with water and sprinkling the same water on their (respectors) head. The place of son-in-law in Rajbanshi community is equal to the son. Father-in-law, mother-in-law and other respectable persons of that side should be saluted by the son-in-law touching his forehead on their toes. Kith and kins and the relatives use to be carefully treated in this community. The salutation and traditional formalities are carefully followed while meeting each other. Otherwise there will be the danger of the presence of social criticism.

Social Relations:

The root of the social values, norms and traditions in Rajbanshi community is too strong. There is the main control of society in all the works and activities to be done on wedding, birth and death culture. Persons to be called or invited and the expenditure amount should be decided according to the type of purification and suggestion given by the society. The decision made by the society must be implemented totally although it may be unfavourable to some of them. While supporting or applying the decision made by the society, if they are unable because of poor economic condition they must borrow or take loan committing to pay a large amount as interest, if not, selling a pair of bullocks, his buffaloes or piece of land they have owned. In this way, they must compulsorily complete the task given by the society, otherwise they use to be socially boycotted being compelled. Some of the conscious and educated Rajbanshi youths have already known that there are some of the spiritual traditions in their community which are as diseases, although they haven't brought any change in them because of the fear of being socially boycotted and bitterly criticised. In this way, in this community there is a great responsibility of each person to respect the Society. In reference to the social relationships the relation of the Rajbanshi's of Jhapa is not limited to their district but also equally spread to the Rajbanshi's of Bengal and Bihar regions of India. Rajbanshi's of Jhapa are more interested to marry with Indian Rajbanshi's instead of inter-caste or same caste marriage within Nepal.

Dresses:

Inspite of having their own distinctive traditional dresses, Rajbanshi's use to wear modern dresses also. The effect of modern dresses seems in male Rajbanshi's whereas it is rare in females. Loin-cloth and shirt (Dhoti and Kamij) are the traditional dresses of male Rajbanshi's. Workers in the field use to wear loin-cloth only. Shirt and loin-cloth, inspite of being formal dresses, the number of short mantlet roller males as loin-cloth is great. Rajbanshi youths who are not unknown about modern dresses use to wear pant, shirt, cloak and trousers, coat, cap etc. The dress of Rajbanshi's seems simple. Items of their dresses are too simple and limited. Rajbanshi women use to roll a wide piece of cloth covering from breast to knees. That piece of cloth mostly have the length of about 2 meters which is called "Petani". The use of Petani is usual together with a bodice and a petticoat. Petani is being made with a thick cloth manufactured in their houses. Women use to wear Petani while at being in their houses as well as going to the market. They use to wear a mantle in winter. Some of the women living near the towns have started to wear a bodice and a sari (Petticoat). Some of the Rajbanshi's use to tell previous stories related to the use of Petani while at being out of sight after escaping towards the jungle because of the fear of Parshuram, they had felt lack of cloth. Anyway they had made thick cloth in the jungle which was used as Petani by the women and loin cloth by men. The same custom became their tradition according to the public or mass concept they have.

Ornaments:

Most of the Rajbanshi men don't wear ornaments except a simple finger ring. Similarly, Rajbanshi women also don't wear more ornaments. They use to wear ornaments made of silver in comparison to gold. Married women always use to wear a silver chain in their necks. There is a tradition of giving silver chain, silver bracelet and silver bangles in wedding. The silver chains being worn on formal occasions do have more weight of about one kilogram to 1250 grams. They don't have the custom of wearing weighty ornaments in legs and arms as in other caste's. The practice of blue Nadina (vaccinatory embroidery) as an ornamental decoration is not among them as in other terrains. In brief, it can be said that the dresses of this caste are too simple.

The use of shoes and sandles has been done only by men of this caste. There is no environment for wearing shoes and sandles in their village. Some of the Rajbanshi's die without wearing shoes and sandles once in their life. Old men mostly use to shave their hair but young boys use to follow modern practice.

Women from Rajbanshi caste don't wear all kinds of ornaments at once. They wear them in fairs and festivals only. There is no keen interest of wearing ornaments in Rajbanshi women. They don't wear 'Tika' (a small caste-mark) on their forehead and also don't wear vermillion on the parting in the hair because they don't make parting while combing their hair.

Now-a-days it is found that some of the modern and educated Rajbanshi young girls use to make parting in their hair and put some vermillion in it.

Rajbanshi women have long, soft and attractive black hair. They use to comb their hair nicely and make a hump (twisted hair) at back. They use to make niches of their hair according to their own interest. There is no woman found in Rajbanshi family who does not comb her hair. They use to use mustard, coconut and other different kinds of oil found in the market. Mostly they use mustard and coconut oil. They don't like to be more ornamented and decorated.

Food:

The main food of Rajbanshi's is rice, pulse (dal) and curry. They don't grow wheat and maize as their crops. Mainly they use to have rice. They use to like steamed rice than unsteamed. Variety of food like sweetmeat made with wheat and maize are being assumed as the cause of making more thirsty and harmful to their health. While at having as tiffin and in different festivals, they use rice-flour to make bread and pancake. The main product of Jhapa is paddy (rice). So, it is being used excessively.

Mostly used sweetmeats made with rice are: bread, murahi, beaten rice and rice prepared from the boiled paddy. Murahi, beaten rice and the rice prepared from the boiled paddy are being used in having tiffin whereas they usually like to have rice, pulse and curry in their lunch and dinner. They use to prepare bread on special occasions, festivals and at the arrival or the presence of their daughters. The next food prepared by this caste is "Panta Bhat". They use to have this especially in summer as their breakfast. They use to put rice in the water at night and the next morning they use to have it adding salt, oil and onion after removing water from it. Such a food is called 'Panta Bhat' which is being used in Rajbanshi society assuming as the longlasting and hygenic tiffin for all.

In addition to the rice, there is the use of pulse, green vegetables and a variety of food made with gram widely. Both the fresh and dry vegetables from jute are being used as their curry. In the food of Rajbanshi's oil, spices and chilly are being used much. Fish and meat of pigeon and goat are their dinner. If they don't be able to purchase fish and meat, most of the Rajbanshi's use to go for fishering to the gathered water in the field, terrains, ponds, lakes and on the banks of rivers.

Rajbanshi's use to tame cattle but they rarely use milk and curd in their food. By selling milk and curd they purchase goods needed in their household like salt, spices and others. They prefer fish and meat in comparison to the milk and curd. But meat is a must in every feast and death feast.

Besides goat, pigeon, duck and fish, there is a tradition of having meat of deer, rabbit and wild animals in Rajbanshi society. They don't like people who eat the meat of hog, buffalo, chicken and have drugs like alcohol etc. In Rajbanshi community, most of them including children, adults, male and female are addicted to betelnut and smoking.

Pots and instruments:

Rajbanshi's use clay pots and metal pots both. Among these pots they buy clay pots from potters and metal pots in the market. Metal pots mean that they are generally made with bell metal and steel. They keep limited number of dishes, cups and glasses in their houses. Therefore, they show their hospitality serving food on the leaf of bananas especially in the feasts.

Metal, alloy, silver, iron and copper made pots have been used from the very beginning by them. Now-a-days they have started to use big dishes for having food, tall brass urn for water (Karuwa), steel glasses and water pots to drink water. In the same way, they use cane mat, oval cushion mat, and bag made of jute (prepared by themselves) to dry rice and it is found that they use winnowing fan, sieve, basket and flower basket etc. to sift and lock up rice. They prepare these things themselves and also buy them.

Weapons:

They use various kinds of weapons for their daily domestic use. Among the weapons they have been using the following are the most: Nepalese sword (Khukri), axe, adze, saw, small prunning knife, open knife, kitchen knife, digging tool, dagger and pore-maker tool etc. Because of being keenly interested in fishering, they mainly use fishhooks and traps. In the same way, they use plough, yoke, plough share, the pole or beam of a plough etc. Among these weapons, they buy weapons made of iron from the market and asking black-smiths to make them, whereas weapons made of wood are being prepared by themselves.

Status of Male and Female in Rajbanshi Society:

It is obvious that Rajbanshi community is being headed by males. There is a custom of next (second) marriage if they don't have son. Similarly, the tradition of having multiwives is being accepted by their society. There is no any authority and ownership of daughters in their fathers' property. By these facts, it is clear that there is the dominance of males in this society. In this society, there is no any restriction of being married with the next husband and widow marriage but their society doesn't accept it as a good activity although women as widows cannot be found in their society. Second marriage of women is not socially been accepted. Such kind of marriage is being greeted as "Sanga Dinu" in their society. According to the social belief, worshipping by the hands of the woman who gets second marriage is neglected although it is not applied in their behaviour. The second wife, or the second husband, is being accepted as the bullocks borrowed from the moneylender promising to pay a certain amount of interest for the purpose of cultivating only. As an example, it is still an obvious tradition, which is found at some of the places, in returning the bullocks borrowed with some corn instead of the interest to be paid to the moneylender. According to the comparative study of this tradition, in past and now-a-days it is proved that this custom was more popular in the past decades and gradually lost later. It is clear from the study that not only life long but also after the death, husbands use to claim their right on their wives.

Inspite of the things mentioned above the status of women in Rajbanshi society is high. Rajbanshi women are being seen as already got rid of economic and social corruption. Their status or position among the house-holders is found as the female house-owners. Wholly, including the economic responsibility of householders, purchasing and selling goods and corn in markets etc. In household activities, Rajbanshi women play fully active role. As there is the necessity of a son in Hindu society, Rajbanshi's also feel the presence of a son compulsory, although there is no difference between the services like nutrious food, looking after and the love provided to the sons and daughters.

Chumana System:

In Rajbanshi society, while at the marriage of the girl, a certain amount of money is being paid from the side of bridegroom to the parents and guardians of the girl as the reward of their previous care of the girl. This sort of money to be paid is called "Chumana". The amount of money, determined by the society, is paid by the guardians of the bridegroom to the guardians of the bride after the date of marriage being fixed. There is no any limitation of the amount to be paid as "Chumana". Bearing the economic status of the bridegroom in mind the society members use to decide the amount of 'Chumana'. It is found that the parentage, appearance and character are also being considered while fixing the amount of 'Chumana'. The main purpose of the amount being paid to the parents of the girl as Chumana is the economic help to the father of the girl to bear the expenditure on the wedding ceremony. The amount given by the parents of bridegroom as Chumana is spent on the feast to maintain the social prestige in inviting all their relatives, families etc. In this way, the family of bride's side is not benefitted personally but by using that amount there will be no lack of anything. The next purpose of 'Chumana' is to celebrate the wedding ceremony lavishly, without lack of wealth. Now-a-days this custom is not found in most of the castes of Jhapa district. This kind of tradition is being followed by the families who do have lack of money. Economically strong and medium class Rajbanshi's are opposed to this custom because they think that Chumana is a daughter selling system. Rich and medium class Rajbanshi families follow the tradition of searching richer family for their daughters' marriage. In this community a new custom of giving cattle, goods, corn etc. as donation, presents and dowry to their daughter and sons-in-law is increasing day-by-day. The socially ugly behaviour of dowry which makes daughters as the economic burden is being started in Rajbanshi community. This tradition is the effect of other castes on them. The tradition of celebrating wedding ceremony is an economic burden in Rajbanshi community. The custom of dowry is increasing more economic burden on them. In comparison to dowry system the Chumana system is rather more behavioural and practical in their society.

Danguwa System (Widow Marriage):

Among the main characteristics of Rajbanshi community, Danguwa system is one. When a Rajbanshi woman becomes widow, she faces the problems of household transactions as well as proper upbringing of her children. In order to solve this problem, widows use to start their new life with the person (male) who is out of her relatives and dynasty. Such a man who becomes the life friend of the widow is called "Danguwa". Inspite of the obvious relations between the widow and "Danguwa" as husband and wife, the woman belongs to her home property and son. The right to give the property including house and land to the children from Danguwa is reserved by the woman. The man living as Danguwa should obey or work according to the direction given by the woman.

Woman who wants to keep a 'Danguwa' should ask or inform her society before keeping Danguwa in her house. Their society accepts it either being informed or not. But the difference is that if the society has already been informed about the man who is going to be kept as Danguwa, the relatives and society members of the woman cover his appearance with a veil and make him enter the woman's house at night. At the time of the Danguwa being entered no unmarried boys are allowed to be there. Most of the men selected as Danguwas come from low income family or economically poor families, whose wife had already died and he is passing life alone etc. No unmarried boys can be kept as Danguwa. Danguwa is being placed physically as the husband of the woman but in reality it is different because he is not being respected equal to the real husband and no ownership is being given to him about household behaviours.

The next symbol of married Rajbanshi women is the use of vermillion and shak (bangle made of small shells) but they don't use and wear them. So their place is being taken as the place of the boss or house owner. There is no prestige of Danguwa in the society. No worshipping and funeral activities are accepted done by him. He is always being hated in the society. There is a customary assertion that the grain of the food given by the Danguwa will not be eaten by the elephant too. The family or the children from the Danguwa are being assumed to be prestigeless in the society.

III

Rajbanshi Life-cycle and Rituals

Birth, entering to the youth and adolescent period, reproduction and death are the natural events of human life. But man, being a cultural creature, accepts the cultural importance of the events of life. Therefore, there is no mankind which doesn't accept the abovementioned difficult situations. Those events use to create and establish new relationship between different individuals and groups. Each other in every human being from which the role and level or status of individuals can be explained. If a child borns in a family, a new relationship is created or established with him or her in his own family as well as related to all the individuals and also the role use to be created or assigned. In the same way, there use to be established a new relationship between the living members of their group when a member of their group dies. In such a way, the cultural value is being given differently in every human society to these events. According to the cultural point of view, they accept these events as the difficult situation found in the related society.

In the life cycle of the Rajbanshi society of Jhapa, the same different difficult situations are being seen, which are being valued in their own way by the culture of that place. But the ways of giving value to some situations among them are different according to the situation and gender which is explained as follows:

(a) Birth Sacrament:

The main purpose of marrying a boy and girl is to increase family members (son or daughter) in their home. The birth of a child in a house invites pleasure and cheerfulness in that family. After being married and having given birth to a child, their real social life begins.

Pregnant women are used to be restricted to do some of the things like to touch, to jump over and to eat. For example, pregnant woman must not do any hard and strength needed work. They also must not cross the big rivers. They don't jump over the ropes used to tie cows, bullocks and horses. They do have a belief that if a pregnant woman jumps over such a rope the child going to be born from her becomes exactly alike with the animal tied with that rope in its character and habits. Similarly, pregnant women don't look at monkeys because of the fear of being their child exactly alike them in their faces. They also use to say that no pregnant women should face towards the sky while at dropping fruits from the trees and the leaves of bananas from their trees otherwise the child going to take birth be facing towards the sky all the time. Because of the fear of ghosts' attack, Rajbanshi pregnant women don't go to the markets and anywhere at a distance. In this stage they don't go to the garden and kitchen garden. The husband of the pregnent women vow for the betterment of their wives and future generation. There is a belief about the children not being alive. In Rajbanshi society if the first child dies they use to make their god worshipped by "Chhumati Gosai" (child's witch doctor who trembles while worshipping) frequently while their wives becoming pregnant for the second time. In this way, Rajbanshi's who lose their first child use to offer the next from the conception period to the Chhumati Gosai and they do have belief that Chhumati Gosai can protect the child by using incantation as the water ridged in a terrace.

Mostly the mother of a woman in child birth lives together

in the same room during this period. If the mother is not available at that time, her mother in-law, husband's elder sister-in-law or experienced neighbour old woman use to live with the woman. They help the woman suffering at delivery. At this time, if they don't have the relative women, the husband also helps in the room of childbirth. In some of the Rajbanshi families there uses to be a midwife in such conditions who is called "Dayani" from 'Hari' caste. After the birth of the child she must cut the naval string of the new baby with a split cane of bamboo. If they don't be able to manage the woman from Hari caste, the grandmother of the new baby uses to cut it. But such a case is rare. If other caste's woman cuts the naval string, she is boycotted from their society.

The members of Hari caste use to say 'Majhi' for themselves on their sub-surname. This caste is also found divided into 2 groups—group 'A' and 'B'. Group 'A' make things and pots with bamboo whereas group 'B' works as Band-player and mid-wife. Both these groups are assumed as the people of low level and no other caste members have things to be touched by them in Rajbanshi Society, but now-a-days they use to eat them. If the naval string of the new baby could not totally be cut from the mother in reasonable time they use to tie the hair hump of the woman by the leather rope used to join the beam of a plough and yoke. Similarly, there is a tradition of throwing a load lifting wooden stick named 'Kara' making the roof-tree crossed. If the problem could not be solved, they call the witch doctor called 'Ojha'.

There is a tradition of causing the woman to sleep in the childbirth on a mat, on the straw or thatch or on the bag made of jute called 'chatai' until she becomes pure. After cutting the naval string they offer the child to the sun. The new baby uses to be kept in a winnowing fan which is called 'Shupa'. Touching the shupa and the well with a rope, they worship the well. While worshipping the well, they put 5 takas in a register outside the well if the baby is male and throw 5 takas of vermillion inside the well if the baby is female. After worshipping, because of the first coming of the child in the world, they put the baby on the winnowing fan and cause to see in all the four directions.

After completion of the formalities mentioned above, the hair of the baby is cut by the barber saving two tufts of hair within 1 or 2 days. The custom of making two tufts of hair, according to Ojha (witch doctor) is that one is cut after the death of the baby's father and the other on the turn of mother. There is particularly no custom of avoiding for the time being a child-birth. There is a custom of being pure within two days according to the household necessities and the condition of the mother as well as of the baby. But generally there is a custom of being pure in ten to eleven days of the childbirth in Rajbanshi Society.

On the day of being pure they need a barber and a priest called 'Adhikari'. Adhikari works as a priest in Rajbanshi society. On that day the barber cuts the hair and nails of all the members of that family. If not cutting the hair they must cut their nails. All the servants too must touch their body with the rajor of the barber. Adhikari uses to sprinkle the rajor cleaned water in all the rooms and on each and every stair of the house. If there is a woman in child-birth in the house of Adhikari, he uses to do all these works herself. All the clothes of that house must be cleaned and the inner courtyard as well as the house must be made pure by smearing them.

There is a tradition of not giving rice, ghee and milk to the woman in childbirth generally up to five days and in some of the places up to 22 days. They give fish, bread, raw sugar and beaten rice to the woman but do not give green vegetables in childbirth.

Naming the Child

There is no any child naming culture found on a fixed day in Rajbanshi Society. Inspite of the prevailing traditional custom of naming the child using calender, but now-a-days most of the Rajbanshi's don't use calender and use to name their child haphazardly and at no fixed time. They do follow various methods while naming their child *e.g.* time, birth day, birth month, some of the main events or joining with the name of their earlier child etc. For example, if a female baby takes birth at the time of dawn, she used to be named as 'Bhokhati' or 'Dinjani'. Similarly, naming on the basis of birth month sons are being named as 'Kartike, Chaitu, Baisakhu, Savniya, Asaru, etc. whereas the daughters are being named as Chaiti, Gauguni, Savni' etc. In the same way, on the basis of important events like 'Land Reform in Nepal', children used to be named as 'Bhumisudhar'. There is a custom of naming the children on the basis of their faces, colour and character too. *e.g.* If the girl is white, she is being named as 'Dudhsari', if she is black she is being named as 'Kali', if the girl becomes angry quickly, she is being named as 'Ansari'. In addition to this tradition, there is a custom of joining the name of the elder brothers with the name of the younger brothers and elder sisters with the younger sisters. For example, if the name of the elder brother is 'Kalu', younger brother's name becomes 'Bhalu' and the next younger brothers names as 'Alu' and so on. In this way the Rajbanshi's use to express diversity and sweetness as well as simplicity in naming their children meaningfully. Some of the rich Rajbanshi's have started to use the calender and are using modern names while naming their children.

There is also a peculiar custom of naming their children; if the baby of a Rajbanshi takes birth and die soon, the name of the future or the next child be bad or hateful. It is because of the hopelessness about the expected lifespan of their children.

(b) Khirchhuwa (Rice Feeding)

In the Rajbanshi community, there is a tradition of rice feeding called Khirchhuwa to their children after birth and within 6 to 8 months. This customary ceremony should be completed before sprouting the teeth of their children. In Rajbanshi society, mostly they use to celebrate 'Khirchhuwa' on the turn of their first child. They use to complete this ceremony greatly and equally without discriminating in son and daughter. There is no custom of Khirchhuwa at the time of the next birth. There is a tradition of worshipping god Satyanarayan, burn offering, muttering repeatedly etc. while celebrating 'Khirchhuwa' for the purpose of prosperity and long life of the child. There becomes a vital role of maternal uncle of the child in Khirchhuwa. If the maternal uncle is not available, Khirchhuwa uses to be completed by the artificial brother made by the mother of the child. In this ceremony, at first the maternal uncle helps his nephew to gargle and feeds rice-pudding and also washes his hands and mouth after feeding. Maternal aunt follows the same after her husband. On this occassion, maternal uncle and aunt give a gift to their nephew. After that grandfather and grandmother of both side, uncle and aunt as well as other relatives should give golden gift. Parents do not eat anything in the house of their daughter until their grandsons and grand daughters start to speak.

(c) Karnachhed (Forming holes in ears):

Marriage ceremony could not take place before the initiation of a child into caste and investiture ceremony with the sacred thread in Brahmin and Chhetries. Similarly, there will be no marriage of the boy who has not completed the 'Karnachhed' custom in Rajbanshi society. There is no any fixed time tradition of completing the 'Karnachhed Custom' in Rajbanshi society. This custom can be completed up to the previous day of being married. Some of them use to complete this custom in childhood, some of them at the time of 'Khirchhuwa', whereas some till the previous day of marriage ceremony. The act of 'Karnachhed' is being done by Thakur. On this occassion, Gosai Thakur uses to cast a spell in ear together with worshipping differently. There is a tradition of assuming purity only after hearing the spell in Rajbanshi society.

The same method is being applied for the son and daughter up to rice feeding (Khirchhuwa). After this the methods are different. Daughters, because of being ear-ring wearers use to be formed holes in their ears at Karnachhed custom. After this, there is no any tradition as 'Ihi and Braha' in Newar community before being married.

No any Rajbanshi lady cares and give importance to the first as well as the later menstruations. Menstruation is entirely a natural thing which is accepted by all. At the time of monthlies, they do not enter into the garden as well as kitchen garden.

The children of Rajbanshi family are assumed as helpful because the boys and girls of being 7/8 years use to help in the household behavioural works. They help their parents and guardians carrying snacks to the family members working in the rice fields and caring their younger brothers and sisters. Because of the effect of other castes, they have started to send their children to schools in their villages. In the spare or leisure time, the Rajbanshi children memorise 'The Holi' or spring festival and they also use to be involved in fishering after going to the streams and rivers.

Childhood is assumed as the happiest time in lives of Rajbanshi's. As the children become young and adult, most of them being dropouts from their school and are engaged in their household works and occupations of their family. At the time of youth the most important culture is wedding ceremony which will be described in a separate title.

In the society having fatherhood, the eldest son becomes the main source of all the responsibilities after the death of his father. Inspite of having the difference in age, all the brothers share their father's property equally. On the occassions of feasts and festivals, respectful feelings are shown in accordance with the seniority of their age. Similarly, in Rajbanshi community the relation between brothers and sisters use to be close. Sisters married and gone to others' houses mostly expect love and more help from their brothers. Going to the houses of the married sisters frequently and exchanging good wishes to each other is assumed as the duty of the brothers.

In Rajbanshi community, as they grow older, they suffer from inferiority complex. They must do hard labour in old age too, if they were not able to save money in time whereas they become weak at this time. These people use to do hard work as much as they can in old age too. They become dependent upon their sons and daugthers only after being totally unable to do the work. The life-span of old people seems to be 60 to 70 years on an average.

(d) Marriage custom:

Among the ordinary characteristics of human beings of the world, marriage is one. Marriage, not only provides social recognition to the physical and sexual relation between the married couple but it also explains the co-relation between the married couple together with their family, clan and relations including all the social relationship established newly and acts as directing to it. Inspite of being the marriage custom all-pervading, the marrying methods are not similar and the same are more than one in the same caste too. In some of the communities, there is no need of marriage to provide the social value for the sexual relation. In such a community, the purpose of marriage is not providing the social value to the sexual relation but keeping the social organization going on.

In the marriage custom of the Rajbanshi's of Jhapa, there are some of the customs as found in Hindu tradition whereas their own castewise originality is being found at some places. In this community, while marrying, they marry the persons next to their blood relation. No marriage can be done between maternal uncle's children and father's sisters' children. There is a rule to be followed while marrying *i.e.* 7 (seven) generations from the side of the father and 5 generations in preceptor's family and making next to the 3rd generation in the family of a formal friend relationship. They must marry each other although these rules are not completely followed by themselves. They don't marry within their blood relatives if they use to be noticed themselves.

There are various techniques of marrying in Rajbanshi caste. Among them arranged marriage, Ghainjiya, Dumdume and Danguwa marriage are the main ones. Besides these, now-a-days at some of the places, some of the adult youths have love-marriage. From the point of view of social value, the most usual and the best marriage custom is arranged marriage. Marrying after the agreement made between bride-bridegroom's side is called arranged marriage.

In the wedding ceremony of Rajbanshi caste, they use to take different things from 7 castes' people *e.g.* flower from the gardener, Bingnu (fan) made by Dum (tailor), basket or winnowing fan made by Handi, similarly curd from a milkman, beaten rice from Gaingai, razor of a barber and kahars are being used to lift and carry the Palanquin. From this activity, the abilities and the works to be done by different castes are being justified.

The following methods and the things to be done are followed by Rajbanshi's from initiation to the end.

(*a*) Suba Dekha:

While marrying according to the traditional customs, is the first traditional activity in Rajbanshi community. In this tradition, when the son or the boy becomes mature (more than 16 years), the persons from the side of the bridegroom start search for a girl (bride). When they find a girl in an acceptable living standard and matured (more than 12 years), they assign a man to work as a Kahuwa (match maker) and send him to the house of the girl in order to talk and bring information about the day and the place to be fixed for seeing the girl either being in the girl's house or vise versa. On the day fixed by them, the father of the boy or the uncle from the father's side goes to the house of the girl together with Kahuwa and one or two his relatives. The persons from the side of the girl use to clean their house and courtyard on that day. They welcome people from the side of the boy with warm hospitality on arrival. They use to greet or salute the guests sitting outside the girls house which uses to be beautified well at that time. On this occasion, the father of the boy looks at the palms of the girl putting a present or some money on them. In the meantime, there is a tradition of asking the girl her name and other things to be noticed about the sound and good as well as proper behavioural manners. After this act, people from the side of the boy return back to their house. If the family, living standard and the manners, as well as behaviour are all with melevolent stars, Family Thakurs behaviour is according to their intention, they send Kahuwa to the house of the girl to inform about the acceptance of this relation. While returning back from the house of the girl,

Kahuwa relays complete details about the acceptance or the rejection of the proposal by the parents of the girl to the father of the boy.

(*b*) Dulha Tilkhibar:

After getting the information about 'Suba Dekha' from the side of the boy, if the persons from the side of the girl want to see the boy and his house as well as his living standard at the same time they send the message by the medium of Kahuwa about the date for being in the house of the boy as in Dulha Tilkha. Kahuwa, coming in the house of the boy from the house of the girl, informs the date of Dulha Tilkha including the time and the number of persons going to be involved in it. On the day fixed for this purpose, the father of the girl or the guardian reach the house of the boy with some persons. The father and other persons of the boy show warm hospitality to the guests coming from the side of the girl. The father or the guardian of the girl, giving a present in the hands of the boy, use to ask some questions to him in order to find out his character, manner and abilities. After that, returning back to their house, they send the message about the acceptance or rejection of the proposal by the medium of Kahuwa. If they like the boy, his standard of living, character and behaviour, the father or the guardian of the girl gives betelnut to the father of the boy as a symbol of acceptance for marriage. This tradition, in Rajbanshi community, is being named as 'Suberpan'.

(*c*) Pan Katani:

After agreement between the parents of the boy and the girl, suberpan takes place, only after that other activities of the marriage take place respectively. After the end of the Suberpan, the persons from the side of the bridegroom send a message through Kahuwa to the persons related to the bride about the date for being in Pan Katani. On that day, persons on the side of the girl stay in the house being prepared for this purpose. On the day fixed, there is a tradition of giving 300 to 900 betels and nuts in accordance with their capacity by the persons from the side of the boy when coming to the house of the girl with kahuwa to the persons of the girl's side. These betels and nuts are given to the persons on the side of the girl for the purpose of the functions like Egana Khechani, Suba Dekhani and Garam Sewa etc. If the persons from the girl's side refuse to take these betels and nuts there is no any compulsion from the boy's side to give.

(*d*) Daiguwa (Dalikhara):

After the completion of Pankatani, Daiguwa comes next. Rajbanshi's use to say Dalikhara too to Daiguwa. Some of the persons from the side of bridegroom determine the date of Daiguwa or Pan Katani and inform the girl's side. But some of them send the message about the day fixed for Daiguwa to the girl's side after discussing themselves by the medium of kahuwa. In the marriage custom of Rajbanshi community it is not assumed as guarranted about the marriage until the Daiguwa being completed on the day fixed. Already a fixed number of persons from the side of bridegroom go to the house of the bride as guests. All the paiches (assembly) use to assemble there. On this occasion Kahuwa uses to prepare the betelnut of Dalikhara. After the preparation of the betelnut they have some food and edible varieties. Then they make sit in the courtyard the persons from the side of bridegroom and they make the bride sit in front of the guests. After that, from the side of the bridegroom, the father of the bridegroom or his guardian gives the dresses, ornaments etc. to the bride as much as possible. The persons, as the guests gone to the house of the girl from the side of the bridegroom also give presents to the bride at the same time. Persons from both the sides take an account of the dresses and ornaments given to the bride as presents in detail. The father of the bride and other guardians of her should keep those different things safely as pledge because all these things should be carried back towards the house of the bridegroom after the marriage. After the completion of these formalities to be done the persons of bridegroom's side return back to their houses. If they decide the date of marriage immediately, they decide the auspicious time for the performance of the wedding ceremony on the day of Daiguwa. If not, Karalibhar and Sandos etc. customs remain to be completed.

(*e*) Sandos:

The gift or the present of edible things, used to be given to the mother or other guardians of the bride in return to the care taken and support given by them from the side of the bridegroom, is called Sandos. On the day of Daiguwa, people assembled from the side of the girl talk with the persons from the boy's side about feeding or not feeding Sandos. If the persons of the boy's side want to be feeded, they use to come to the girl's house one day as guests with fish, meat, sweets, milk, curd etc. showing a great fashion to them. In Rajbanshi community feeding Sandos is being conceptualized as respect to the near relatives.

(*f*) Karali Bhar:

In Rajbanshi community, Karali Bhar means the act of sending the message about fixed day for the auspicious moment to the house of the girl. Now-a-days this tradition is being followed on the same day of Daiguwa. In the past time and now-a-days too, after completing Daiguwa they remain silent for a long time and later on they can establish the marital relation with each other. Mostly, in such a case only, they feel the need of Kahuwa from the boy's side for the purpose of sending the message to the girl's side about the Karali Bhar. There is a tradition of assuming that half of the marriage between the boy and the girl has already been completed after the end of Daiguwa in their community. There is also the tradition and provision of marrying after 2 or 3 years of Daiguwa. If the girl dies in this gaping priod between Daiguwa and the main wedding ceremony, the boy should be involved in mourning. Similarly, vise versa of it is being found in case of the boy too and the girl be assumed as a widow." The girl who is involved in Daiguwa cannot be married to others" is the social rule of Rajbanshi's.

(g) Adibas:

The previous day of being in the bridegroom's procession in the house of the bridegroom is called Adibas. This day is assumed as the first day of the marriage. In the marriage of the Rajbanshi caste, after the completion of Karali Bhar, Adibas, Bairati Gaman and Bharbhat are the mentionable days in their tradition.

On Adibas, all the gods and goddesses are worshipped in the house of the girl. Friends as well as relatives come from different places and far distances. On this day, the girl (bride) establishes new and very close friendship with the girl liked by her. The feast used to start widely since the day of Adibas in Rajbanshi Community. On the same day the elder sisters of the girl use to apply the paste made with Kasakuta mixing some oil, on the girl's body. Kasakuta be made with turmeric powder and Kasa (a kind of marsh-growing plant) beating and mixing some oil in it.

On Adibas, all the activities to be performed and the environment on the side of the bridegroom are also the same at the girl's house. On this day, they use to worship Matsya and Satya Narayan, their clan gods (Kul Thakur, Satguruwa, Ramaut, Thuthuniyan, etc.). The worship of the family god is done by the Gosai Thakurs in Thakurbadi together with other gods. Making sacred the bridegroom also being done by Gosai Thakur. On the occasion of the worship there used to be the presence of Kirtiniyas. At night, the grandmother of the house or the elder sister of the mother roast Kasakuta and the married elder sister or elder sisters-in-law rub the mixture of Kasakuta adding some oil all around the body of the bridegroom. There is a concept that Kasakuta is for the purity of mind and body in their community.

On this occasion, the elder and younger brothers-in-law of the boy wearing new cloth round their waists, make 'Maruwa Khuda' to young and old respectively. 'Maruwa Khuda' means to dig a pit where there is planted a banana plant. This act is done in the courtyard. At the time of Maruwa Khuda the elder and younger brothers-in-law by their younger and elder sisters-in-law and other women splash and spatter turmeric powder, colour, water, curd etc. and also rubbing black-soot to them. They tease and make dishonour to them. After such an interesting scene, ocassionally, they entertain each other. This being over than the limitations too like teasing, using their parts of the body, splashing whatever they get and enjoying the delightful environment etc. After the preparation of Maruwa Khuda, making the bridegroom sit in it, the Nawa Thakur (barber) shaves the hair and cuts nails of the bridegroom. In this way, for making sacred the bridegroom, his married elder sisters and the elder sisters-in-law rub Kasakuta all over his body. If they are supposed to be in a marriage procession at a distance, the next day's act of worshipping called 'Am Mahalaune' be completed by the bridegroom. Am Mahalaune, in Rajbanshi community, is the special tradition of worshiping the mango tree wrapping 5 times to it with a crude thread. The bride also does the same in her house after the arrival of the marriage procession. During the night of Adibas, the bridegroom exchanges Dhoti (a kind of cloth to wear round the waist) and betelnut as well as making the different god and goddesses witness, he establishes the relation of Mistar to a friend of his own caste and community. There is a little bit difference between Mit and Mistar. Mit is not allowed to look at the face of the wife of his Mit but this rule is not applied in case of Mistar who uses to be a witness of the marriage of the bridegroom.

Bairati or Chapahari
(Persons involved in a marriage procession):

The next day to Adibas and the day on which the marriage procession takes place, is called the day of 'Bairati'. On this day, in the morning, Gosai Thakur takes the bridegroom to their family god and makes him sacred by speaking some vedic text in his ear. If the work of worshipping the mango tree is left to be completed, they perform it first. Then the bridegroom is made completely sacred after rubbing Kasakuta all around his body.

Just after the completion of the activities mentioned above, the bridegroom have food sitting together with the persons who are ready to go in the marriage procession. Because of the task of presenting vermillion on that night time, the bridegroom uses to have other varieties of food except corn, salt and oil. After having food, the bridegroom is worn Kurta (a kind of shirt) or vest and Dhoti together with wrapping a red coloured 7, 9 or 16 hands lengthened turban round his head according to his choice. The Kurta and Dhoti should also be made red. After beautifying the bridegroom, he is given a knife in which there is kept a nut on its tip. It is called a life-knife by the Rajbanshi's which remains in the hand of the bridegroom until the completion of the marriage.

After the end of the activities mentioned above persons involved in the marriage procession go to the house of the bride. The bridegroom is taken in a palaquin. Marriage procession goes by well decorated and beautified bull and buffalo-carts together with a group of instruments players. They have their own kind of instruments. Among them, the special ones are: Tansi, Sahenai, Rukhuri, Thenthaini, etc. On the way, when they pass through the places of Hindu gods and goddesses the bridegroom gets off and worships them all.

Towards the side of the girl, on this day, all the persons who are required to clean the feet or be involved in presenting the girl to the bridegroom, have their food except corn, salt and oil. From time to time, the friends of the girl, who is going to be the bride or other young girl's use to sing different songs in their group. In the house of the bridegroom too, it is found that young girls of Rajbanshi caste sing some of the group-songs occassionally from the night of Adibas. In both kinds of songs there may be the reflection of striking satires on social disorders whereas in some songs there may be the flow of pathos. Mostly the songs, being sung by Rajbanshi young ladies, specially in the wedding ceremony, reflect insult and abuse to each other in their own way, particularly from the side of bride to the bridegroom side persons and vice versa. The most important rationale of doing so is the restriction of criticizing, rating and abusing behaviours between the relatives to each other after being joined in marital relationship. Therefore, they use to insult, abuse and criticise each other before the end of the marriage by the medium of songs and civilized words as they can express.

When the marriage procession reaches in the village of the bride, the children of her side hinder their way just before their arrival which is called 'Ghat Teknu', the group of children ask for betelnut and some money. Persons from the side of the bridegroom use to satisfy that group of children and go ahead. In fact 'Ghat Teknu' means to stop the marriage procession with their palanquin stopping them to go ahead. When the procession reaches at the main gate of the bride's house, a group of young women stop the bridegroom singing different kinds of satiric songs. The bridegroom also gets off there, where the younger sisters of the bride worship the feet of the bridegroom and also clean them with water. Then the elder brothers-in-law of the bridegroom lifts him and carries towards the place meant to make the guests and the persons involved in the marriage procession sit, where the bridegroom accompanies them to be seated. Persons from the side of the bride do come at the place and clean the feet of the persons in the marriage procession including the bridegroom. After having the dinner by the guests, making the bride sit in the palanquin, they carry her towards their family (clan) god and other gods as well as goddesses for the purpose of worshipping together with the playing of bands.

On the other rside the Maruwa Khuda (elder brothers-in-law) of both sides make a pavilion for ceremonial purpose (Jagge) planting the banana trees. At first they make the bridegroom sit in that pavilion. Then the relatives of the bride being inside the house pull the bride vigorously and carry towards the pavilion and make her sit. At that moment the bride uses to weep loudly. It is being seen as a usual tradition among them. There uses to be the use of a veil on the bride's head. After making the bride and the bridegroom sit in the Jagge pavilion, the main materials for the marriage ceremony like betel nut, kiya, kur, kasai, Gosain, vermillion, Khuchi, Kori (cowry), mirror, comb, a small earthen lamp, Kalash (a metallic vessel with a narrow neck), leaves of mango, banana, rice and paddy etc. are carried there. Then the marriage ceremonial activities begin.

First of all, the bride and the bridegroom cover a dozyn of bananas with their veils in front of them separately. The elder or younger brother of the bridegroom's father use to make the bride and the bridegroom wear a Chhat on their head. The Chhat is also being called coronet or a flower. It really seems like a crown because there are different decorative ornaments sticked all around it. Such a crown uses to be big for the bridegroom and vice versa of it for the bride. After wearing the Chhat, a barber cuts and cleans the nails of the bride and making the Tarain priest read avowal the parents and guardians of the bride offer as a virgin gift while the bridegroom also presents vermillion. There is no any sacrifice or a burnt offering in the marriage of Rajbanshi's. Only at the time of presenting different gifts, particular lines of avowal are pronounced by the Terain priest. While presenting the vermillion as a gift by the bridegroom to the bride, the bridegroom stands infront of the bride and puts a betel on a Gorsan (a kind of abuse) with some vermillion and by taking the help of a Khuchi (a small stick-stand of cane) he puts the vermillion 3 times in the parting of the hair of the bride. He doesn't touch the vermillion with his hands. After these activities the bride and the bridegroom are given different presents worshipping them with paddy by the relatives of the bride's side. Such a tradition of presenting gifts is called 'Chumaunu' in Rajbanshi Society. On this occassion the grandmother and the elder sisters-in-law feed betel and they also make the environment interesting, making the new couple play cowy.

While performing all the different activities mentioned above there use to be the rise of morning. In such a way a marriage comes to end. This day is being called the day of 'Bharbhat' on the side of bridegroom and saying 'Goodbye day' on the side of bride.

On this morning, the bridegroom is feed the rice pudding in the house of the bride including 'Maruwa Khuda'.

Rajbanshi's use to say 'Khir-khilan' to it. At the time of Khir Khilan, the bridegroom doesn't touch the rice-pudding taken out of the pot for him by his hands immediately. He demands his favourite thing or object and he doesn't have the rice pudding until his demand becomes fulfilled from the side of father-in-laws' house. On this occassion, the sisters-in-law of the bride including grandmother and elder sisters entertain rubbing the soot and flowing the colours to the Maruwa Khuda (the brothers-in-law of the bride and the bridegroom's side) while eating rice pudding. After feeding all the persons involved in the marriage procession the bride is sent under compulsion. Both the bride and the bridegroom use to be seated in the same palanquin. Both the bride and the bridegroom must compulsorily worship the gods, temples found on the way to the bridegroom's house while returning back from the house of the bride's father.

Bharbhat (Feast of Love):

On this day, in the house of the bridegroom, persons for chumaunu (presenters and blessers) come continuously from early in the morning. All the guests come, use to be seated, cleaning their feet with water in a respectful manner. There is a tradition of feeding the persons coming and going fashionably. In the house where feast feeding takes place, first of all a sheet of cloth is spread out and around and in front of it a leaf of banana is spread out with a glass of water too. Many guests use to be seated and feeded atonce and together. Kamkari's (food distributor women) use to put Dal (pulse), rice, curry and pickle as well as meat on those banana leaves. Always Rajbanshi's deal out their food with their hands. They don't use Dadu, Panyu (scoops) and spoons. After dealing the food out, one of the relatives of the bridegroom requests the guests for having the food. Then they have the food given. They don't chat while having their food which has become their tradition. After the completion of having their food, the same person who had greeted earlier to start, comes over there and greets them again for the funishing that feast. After having the food, the guests are respected by offering out betel, nut, cigerettes etc.

Providing warm hospitality in Rajbanshi's community is a great formality. On the day of Bharbhat, the act of having food takes place all the day. On the other side, the marriage procession also use to return to their house in their own way. The procession is stopped at the main gate of the house after arrival. At the same time, being stopped over there, bands used to be played. The palanquin with the bride and bridegroom uses to be put over there. The mother and younger sisters of the bridegroom come over there with water in a metallic vessel with a narrow neck, for chalni-bati. Chalni-bati is a winnowing fan in which paddy, oil lamp, metallic water vessel, leaf of mango, kiya, mirror, comb and betelnut are kept in. The younger sister of the bridegroom cleanse the feet of the bride and the bridegroom with water puting the Chalni-bati in front of them. The mother of the bridegroom uses to chumaunu them at that time as her blessings. Then both of them are seated in Kohabara. (Kohabara is the room for the bride and bridegroom). After a moments rest the bride and the bridegroom use to be seated in the courtyard where Maruwa had been burried, heading towards east. All the guest come over there and give their presents and blessings while sprinkling water with paddy and a leaf of mango.

At the end of Bharbhat, there is a tradition of feeding the Painch (the gentlemen of the village), Tahaluwas (relatives helping in the wedding) and the neighbours of their village. The bride deals out a little Dal-Bhat to them. Likewise the bridegroom deals out the curd. Only after that other varieties of food are dealt out. The rice mixed with pulse and juice of meat or the yellow rice is cooked adding turmeric in it. But the Rajbanshi's say 'Lal Bhat' to this rice. There is also a tradition of avoiding the leftouts (remainings) of the food by the bridegroom at the end. In the evening of Bharbhat, all the Gosai Thakurs, Kirtiniyas, barbers and band players depart to their houses.

Basya Beha:

On the day next to Bharbhat, there is a tradition of making the bride and bridegroom seated in the courtyard and rubbing oil on their head as well as rubbing the Kurakasa on their bodies. Just after this the bridegroom by his elder brothers-in-law and the bride by the elder sisters or elder sisters-in-law of the bridegroom are carried for having a bath which is called 'Basya Snan'. Then both the bride and bridegroom are made to sit in the courtyard again and activities already done on the night of marriage day in the house of the bride like making the Cowry dice played as well as the game named kiya opening and closing are repeated. Because of being the act of repeating the already performed activities in the house of the bridegroom, it has been called 'Basya Beha' or stale marriage.

Ghar Bas:

According to the custom of Rajbanshi's, most of the bride and bridegroom are given the facility of Gharbas since the day of marriage or next to it., Gharbas means the bride and bridegroom being slept in a single room together. Some of the Rajbanshi's make this provision for the bride and bridegroom after the completion of 'Athubari' or after the bride comes back again from her parent's house after 'Sagani Magana'. Athubari and Sagani Mangana are being explained in detail in the pages below. There is also a tradition of worshipping for the deep affection of the bride towards the husband's house after giving the chance of Gharbas.

Athubari:

Assuming the 1st day to Adibas, the eighth day is being called 'Athubari'. In the marriage system of Rajbanshi caste, Athubari is also a special custom. There is a tradition of accompanying the bride by her 4/5 women relatives and children while returning back carrying the bride or on the day the persons involved in marriage procession returning back. They are called 'Dani Aune'. Those Danis use to live together with the bride up to the Athubari day. Kamkaris, Tahaluwas and other near relatives often live in the place of the house where marriage-ceremony had been celebrated upto that day. Particularly, on the day of Athubari, Rajbanshi's use to throw the chhat or coronet already made wear by the bride and bridegroom on the marriage night. Kasaroasted stove, the banana tree or buried Maruwa, things remained and going to be wasted bought for marriage like bananas, curd, milk and food are offered to an idol etc. in the river. Also the bride and bridegroom go to the river with them, and bridegroom at right and the bride at left, holding their hands together, both of them use to take a dip in the river together and carry a palmful of sand in the other hand. While looking towards the palmful of sand, if there are many pebbles seen in one's hand, he/she will get fame and if there is more sand than pebbles he/she will not get fame according to their traditional concept. They keep the sand in their palm and bring it their house and have a bathe. Soap is not allowed to be used while having a bath. After the completion of having a bath and washing the clothes being sacred at the bank of the river, they use to worship simply and return back to their house having some beaten rice, curd and the food offered to the idol.

Sagani Mangana:

After the completion of Athubari, some of the guests called mehman come to carry the bride from her maternal house and also they carry her. Danies who had come together with the persons involved in the marriage procession also returns back with them. On the eighth day from next to the Athubari day, the bridegroom and some women relatives of his, go to bring the bride back. In Rajbanshi community, it is called 'Sagani Mangana'.

Madar Katani:

In Rajbanshi community, in the month of Bhadra (August-September) of the marriage year, the bride must live in her maternal house. This tradition is called Madar Katani. The relatives of the bride from her maternal home use to come and carry her at the end of the month of Shrawan.

Shesh Bidagi:

After completion of Shesh Bidagi, the process of marriage

in Rajbanshi community comes to an end. Shesh Bidagi is the last farewell from the maternal side of the bride. On that day, the dowries left to be given to the daughter and son-in-law from the side of father-in-laws house in the wedding ceremony are given. Likewise the relatives of the bride who couldn't come to the wedding ceremony or being present but had not given presents, give at that moment. Shesh Bidagi, in Rajbanshi community, is being mostly seen just after the Madar Katani whereas someone do it also after 2/3 months.

Various Kinds of Marriages:

There are also other miscellaneous customs of marriage in Rajbanshi community. They are: Damdume, Dhenjiya and Danguwa. If the economic condition of the girl's parents is too poor, there is a tradition of bringing the girl in the boy's house and marry later. Also after the birth of children, marriage can be done. Such a marriage is called 'Damdume marriage'. Likewise, Rajbanshi's make the favourite boy live in their house as a son-in-law for the daughter. It is called 'Dhenjiya Marriage'. Such a house son-in-law must do all the behavioural work in the house according to the order of the father-in-law as well as mother-in-law. The men who wants to live in the father-in-law's house, is to be married there. The third, the tradition of living as a Danguwa is different one. In such marriage, a man who is called Danguwa, lives in the house of a widow as equal to her husband. There is no any rule and regulation of marriage in it.[1]

(e) Death Rites (Purification):

The last stage of humanlife is death. At this time, not only natural change in human living soul occurs but from the cultural point of view the roles of living persons and the dead one as well as the social beliefs are to be re-explained. In each and every caste the stage of death is culturally important for the acceptance of natural norming to this re-explanation.

---

1. See chapter II about Danguwa Marriage (Widow Marriage), p. 53-54.

In Rajbanshi community, death rites are found in accordance with Hindu tradition. They use to burn or bury the corpse. They use to bury the teethless infant children's dead body and in such a condition they don't purify them. They purify themselves for 3 to 5 days according to the age of the dead children who had teeth. Matured persons' corpse is burried or burned according to their own interest. Young boys and young girls corpses are burned in order to be restricted from the frequent memory created by the scene of the grapes. As same to the Hindu religion the eldest son of the dead person burns a thread lamp in the corpse's mouth which is called "Dagbatti", but all the sons could not be compelled to be involved in the obsequies on their father's or mother's death in Rajbanshi society. On the fourth day of buried/burned corpse the son involved in obsequies can transfer the rest of the responsibilities about purification to anyone of his brothers in his own dynasty.

In Rajbanshi society, dead body (corpse) uses to be bathed and worn white clothes by the sons and also make the corpse sleep keeping the head of the dead body towards north in their courtyard. After completion of this work, they use to inform the neighbours, relatives and mourners of the funeral. The mourners do not come until they are called inspite of getting information about it. After the arrival of the mourners, all of them offer coins to the dead body. Then all of them use to make together. After making the corpse slept on the funeral pyre they use to cover it with a white cloth called 'Kafan' and carry it tying well. While lifting the funeral pyre from the courtyard, they all use to pronounce the name of the god 'Bishnu' in one tone and sound together with the blowing sound of shell. In this way, they carry the corpse towards the bank of a river. Either burn or bury whatever they do, the mourners carry a spade and a flat bottomed earthen pot called 'Handi'. A group of men goes together with the corpse. Also the women from the dynasty of the dead person being grouped separately use to go to the bank of the river called 'Ghat' with a flat bottomed earthen pot full of stirred dungcakes with some water and spattering it with a mop turning backside frequently together with their mourns (weepings). They curse to call this flat bottomed earthen pot as "Dukher Handi". They smash it in about the middle place between the house and the bank of the river and bathe going the river.

After reaching the bank of the river the mourners carrying the dead body make a pit in harmony with the size of the corpse if they decide to bury it. After making the pit, the pit digger uses to enter into the pit once and comes out. They make the dead body sleep keeping the head towards north and use to burn a small earthen lamp at the side of the head of the corpse. After this, the person who takes 'Halka', offers three palmful of soil into the pit first and all of them throw soil on the corpse until it comes to the level of the ground. In Rajbanshi society, the person who is the mourner, tie a small piece of cloth in his neck taken from the cover cloth of the corpse (katro) which is called 'Halka' and it is a symbol of a mourner.

If it is decided to burnt the corpse, they use to make the dead body sleep keeping the head towards north on the bank of the river on the pile of wood and they pore pure ghee and oil on it. After that the mourners spatter 3 palmsful of soil in it and lits the funeral fire. After burning or burying the corpse all the mourners have a bathe in the river and according to the direction given by the 'Kantha Thakur' they have food and water. Then they put a square sized piece of white cloth on the ground and hammer one nail on each corner of it and put a flat bottomed earthen pot full of water under it. Then they make holes with the tip of a sickle all around the flat bottomed earthen pot. After that they measure the length of the spade with a barkless stick of jute and they break it into small pieces. Then they bring the spade towards their house.

The women also have a bath and use to offer water uttering the name of the dead. Simultaneously they use to shatter three small pieces of sticks and throw them into the river and while returning back to their houses they use to carry some sand from the river bank. While returning back to their home, the main actress, daughter-in-law of the dead, uses to write three lines with a sickle on the way and also they guide the dead body to go to certain place they had named. While naming the place guiding the dead body to go there, they determine and tell the name of the place at a distance silently. While returning the mourners go towards their houses from the bank of the river, and the persons involved in obsequies give signals with a spade for the purpose of guiding the dead body in the three places on the way as done by the group of women. In the main door (entrance) of their house, fire in dry dung cakes and water in a pot is being kept on this day. All the persons who had gone to the bank of the river with the dead body must clean their feet with the water and must touch the fire kept in the door before entering their houses.

Tin Sinan (The Third Day's Purification Ceremony):

On the third day after the corpse buried or burnt, a purification ceremony is performed which is called 'Tin Sinan'. Rajbanshi's use to invite all their relatives and "Kirtiniyas", who sing hymn on this day. In Rajbanshi society they are skillful hymn singers from the same caste. In most of the cultures of Rajbanshi caste, the presence of Kirtiniyas is assumed as compulsory. On this day, the house of the dead person should be smeared and smoothered with mud over walls and floor which is called 'Sudhabad'. The sons-in-law of the dead use to mix the leaves of the tree Aegle Marmelos with oil cakes in their courtyard and bit them. If there is no any son-in-law, the sisters of the dead person use to do so. Inspite of being the simple meaning of Tin Sinan as to have a bathe going to the crematorium after the third day of cremation, the purifying activities to be done in cremation-ground fall in it.

While going to the cremation-ground Kirtiniyas use to play tombs, symbals etc. and also sing hymns. Sons of the person involved in the purification also go to the cremation ground together with Kirtiniyas and neighbours as well as relatives carrying the materials like oil-cake, small earthen lamp, ghee, banana, milk, betal leaf and nut in a flower-basket. After reaching the cremation-ground, a barber shaves the hair of the sons of the dead person. One who does not shave the hair must cut the nails compulsorily. After this, all of them have a bathe using or rubbing oil cakes as soap. The sons change the pieces of cloth worn on the day of cremation. After these activities, the sons or the persons involved in purification, take water in a waterpot and go to their houses spatting the water on the way. Before entering their houses, they should clean their feet with water and also they should touch the fire in dung-cake, kept at the main entrance of their house.

On this day (Tin Sinan), women in different groups, use to reach the cremation ground weeping and carrying oil-cake, earthen lamp, ghee, banana etc. in a small flower-basket made of cane and called 'Katha'. After having a bath rubing oil cake in their hair, they worship the offerings to manes with the materials carried in the 'Katha'. While returning back to their houses, they use to carry some sand of the cremation ground in Katha. They use to spatter water on the way to their houses while returning. Before entering into their houses, they use to clean their feet with water and touch the fire in dung cakes as done by the sons of the dead person. At last, they use to sprinkle the sand brought from the cremation ground towards the pivot of their houses.

After the completion of the mentioned above activities, they use to make the sons of the dead person stand in the courtyard and use to clean their feet with water and bowdown on their feet as a mark of salutation. After Tin Sinan the sons of the dead person are restricted to be involved in the formality of salutation. On the day of Tin Sinan, all the relatives and invitees use to be fed tea and snacks. The neighbours, relatives, invitees etc. use to carry milk, curd, sugar etc. towards the house of the dead person as a mark of help. Until the completion of all the activities of Tin Sinan, all the persons who have gone to the cremation ground, including family relatives use to be mourning. After Tin Sinan, only the 'Gutiyars' (of the same family) should be mourning.

In the house of the dead person, Adhikari (Rajbanshi priest) use to worship. While worshipping, he sprinkles the razor cleaned water in the whole house. It is most necessary. Only after sprinkling this water the work of Tin Sinan is assumed to be completed.

Death Feast:

After the eighth day of Tin Sinan, there is a tradition of managing a death feast in the name of the dead person. If the eighth day is Tuesday, they use to organise the death feast on the 9th day. It is found that the mourning activity is mainly being followed upto twleve days. If we add "Dhemali" (the last memorization) it seems as 13th day, but because of being free after 12 days, the mourning days are being assumed only upto 12 days.

On the day of death-feast, all the traditional worshipping activities done by the sons of the dead person and the group of women at the cremation ground and in Tin Sinan, are done in more detail. Otherwise all the activities cope with the activities done in Tin Sinan. Finishing, the work to be done in cremation ground when the mourners and others return back to their houses, the Maithili priest makes them involve in "Panchdani" (a kind of gift). But this traditional activity is not being followed by all except rich-families.

Besides these activities, there is a custom of making an ox free if the dead person is from a rich family. There is also a tradition of making the Kantha Thakur (Terain Priest) eat the things offered to the dead person which is called "Katto" giving some money to him. Rajbanshi's use Kantha Thakur only in the work to be done in crematorium. Except this, the death feast, organized in the name of the dead person, is another importance of this day. For the help of the death feast, daughters and sons-in-law including grandsons and grand-daughters, as well the different distant relatives use to come to the house of the dead person bringing castrated and uncastraed goats, curd, milk etc. Necessary things for the feast are managed on behalf of the family of the dead person too, who feed meat, rice, curd and beaten rice etc. varieties respectfully to all. On the feast night, different varieties of edible things are offered to the dead person as putting them on the leaf of banana naming the dead person and the next day early in the morning before the sound of the cock, they are used to be thrown at a distance from their village. The next, on this night, the Thakur (a kind of Rajbanshi hymner), uses to send the soul of the dead person from there, uttering different vedic texts at last. Rajbanshi's use to say 'the soul sending' to it.

On the 13th day of the death, Dhemali is being done. Only after the completion of Dhemali, the death rites are being assumed as entirely completed. Some say "Dhaimali' to 'Dhemali' which means the last memorization and activity custom in the name of the dead person. On this day all the respectable persons of the village use to be involved in the feast as the tradition of 'Dhemali'. On the Dhemali day, first of all they use to smear the courtyard for holiness and they put some turmeric, water, milk etc. there. All the sons, sons-in-laws and neighbours including relatives use to go 5 times around this place and sleeping as prostrated, they give 'Dhemali'. On this occassion, Gosai Thakur (priest of the clan god) utter the vedic texts. The Rajbanshi's of the eastern side say 'Gakhari Diwar' to 'Dhemali'. After this all the persons involved in the feast and the Dhemali offer money as gift to the Kirtiniyas, Gosai Thakur and the barber according to their economic capacity.

There is no any custom of the funeral ceremony performed one year after the death of the person mourned in Rajbanshi's as is in Brahmin and Chhetri castes. The custom of offering water, food etc. to the Brahmans in honour of and for the benefit of manes or deceased ancestors is rarely found among them.

The rules and regulations of the persons involved in obsequies:

The sons of the dead person who are involved in crematorial activities, must tie a piece of cloth in their neck from the last cloth given to the dead person (kafan) and they must be in mourning upto 12 days. During this period, they never use to greet and salute others as for formality. They have food made of unboiled rice. They don't touch or use salt and oil during this period. Persons involved in mourning don't eat banana if the dead person is male and they don't drink milk if the dead person is female. They sit and sleep on a sacred grass called 'Kush' until the end of mourning. They should go to the river daily and do the activities about 'Duki Dahanu' until the death-feast. Duki Dahanu means daily smearing a place of the house from the day next to Tin Sinan and eating rice separating for the dead person from a kind of clay-pot used to cook rice in that very place by the persons involved in mourning. Duki is a clay-pot which should be made to sink into the river everyday. Everyday, they must cook rice in a new Duki.

IV

Economic Status
(Rajbanshi Economy)

Rajbanshi's are being scattered all over Jhapa district. In comparison to the population of central and southern areas of Jhapa, the population in the northern and eastern side is being lower and lower respectively. Before mentioning something about the economic living of Rajbanshi's it will be better to be more clear about the economic status of Jhapa district where they used to live.

The eastern and southern border of it is India, Morang district in the west and district Ilam in the north. It is situated fully in Terai region. In comparison to other districts located in Terai region, in Jhapa the agricultural products like paddy, jute, mustard and pulse are being produced in enough quantity because of the land being more fertile. These products are also being exported in the international market from this place. Specially, the rice and jute are exported to India. Similarly, wood and firewood is also being exported to Indian markets. Therefore, there are many rice-mills and saw-mills here.

There has been established a Solvent (a mill which produces oil from paddy husk) since some years. Similarly, this area is assumed as an economically prosperous area due to the presence of a leaf-cigarette factory and also a jute press.

But the people depending on agriculture are becoming economically poorer day-by-day.

The main trade centres of this area are: Bhadrapur, Damak, Dhulabari, Sanishchare, Buddhabare, Gauradaha, Gaurigunj, Birta, Surunga, Bahundangi, etc. In this very area, Rajbanshi's live on subsistence level both economically and socially. They are also being dominated by other conscious and clever castes. In such a condition, they cannot be forward. There are some economically strong Rajbanshi's too in this community who are also trying to dominate completely the medium and low income groups of their own caste in some places on the basis of intelligence, foul means, education and politics etc. The number of such rich Rajbanshi's is too small in comparison to the medium and low income people. Generally the financial life of Rajbanshi's is simple in status. They are hardly having food in the present context. Among the inhabitants from the very beginning in Jhapa district, Rajbanshi caste seems a ring leader caste. Their lives are being passed in poverty whereas the economic lives of others who are many times simpler than them, like Sadhamal, Satar, Dunuwar etc. can be considered better. Inspite of Rajbanshi's being the upper class inhabitants of Jhapa, except some of their families, most of them are not being able to own the part of land they need due to the following reasons:

(1) Honesty, (2) Thinking intoxication as their aim of life, (3) Not being far-sighted, (4) Lack of Education, (5) Poverty.

In addition to these factors, they fell behind because of the limitation of the land to be owned which had been determined by the Land Reform System in 2021 B.S., because they did not dare to hide their land as had been done by other hilly castes. Some of them had made efforts to hide it but failed. Also the migrants to this hilly region, using their subtlety and consciousness bought the land of Rajbanshi's, persuading and using trickery etc. At many places they had captured the land of Rajbanshi's which is also a reason of the Rajbanshi's being landless. The Rajbanshi's who live in the middle and southern parts have been owning more and enough land in comparison to the Rajbanshi's of the northern area of Jhapa, because there are no other cases of cunning intruders. They remained silent also at the time when others cultivated their land. In this way, the land, owned by them for 50 years living over there had been registered in the name of others which is the obvious example of their simplicity, intoxication and lack of far-sightedness.

(a) Economic Resources

The main occupation of Rajbanshi's is agriculture. They use to depend completely on agriculture in their life. They have been passing their life traditionally having the main profession of agricutlure. They use to be happy to pass their life in the same way in these modern days too. Besides professional agriculture they cannot survive themselves in the present context. The economic resources of Rajbanshi community are limited because of the old and traditional system of agriculture.

The economic life of Rajbanshi's can be studied classifying them under the following heads:

(1) Land (agriculture)
(2) Business (trade)
(3) Animal farming
(4) Labour
(5) Supplementary income sources
(6) Expenditure.

(i) Agriculture

The land is the main permanent property of Rajbanshi's. Most of the Rajbanshi's have a small piece of land only. Some of them, who do not have land, are depending on the land in which they do have tenancy right. Rajbanshi's passing life doing other things except agriculture, are rarely found in their society. On the basis of the nature of the agricultural land, the land is divided in two types:

(a) Meet
(b) Dhanahar

(a) ***Meet land:*** Meet land is the land which is situated a

little higher than others and fit to be settled on it constructing houses and village. This sort of land becomes appropriate for gardening and making vegetable garden as well as growing jute, tobacco and corn (maize) crops too. Because of not being irrigative there is absence of paddy crop. Due to the fear of thief, dacoits and others, Rajbanshi's use to settle in a group of 30/40 families' house together at the same place. Thus the Meet land is suitable for making houses and village rather than being used for cultivation. Such a land is being found too small in comparison to the land Dhanahar.

(*b*) ***Dhanahar land:*** The land which is well irrigative and suitable for producing paddy, is called Dhanahar. It is also being classified as good and bad on the basis of fertility and other qualities. On such a land, the crop of wheat occassionally in the winter, is grown by them together with the production of linseed and the pulse 'Khesari'. Similarly, on the land where the paddy cannot be grown two times, wheat, linseed and Khesari is grown as the winter crop and maize (corn), millet, jute is being produced in summer. But the Rajbanshi's don't like to produce maize, wheat and Khesari much.

The time of cultivating is all around the year although they use to assume the appropriate time for the start, particularly from the month of Chaitra and while at the completion of preparing the crops ready and storing, it generally becomes the time of the end of the month Paush (January). Now-a-days, because of the new tradition of having the wheat crop, all the 12 months are passed on cultivation (agriculture). In this way, inspite of passing the main time of their life on agriculture, the economic status of them is not so good, due to the following reasons:

(*i*) Over expensive nature
(*ii*) Lack of systematic agriculture system
(*iii*) Decreasing quantity of the land owned
(*iv*) Population growth

(*v*) Lack of consciousness about their future, etc.

(ii) Trade (Business)

The Rajbanshi's use to sell only agricultural products like corn, fruits, vegetables, chilly, ginger, turmeric etc. Their area of trade is simple and limited. The women are more skillful than their husbands in trade. They use to sell beaten-rice, Murahi (roasted paddy) and vegetables in the local market and use to fulfill their daily needs like salt, oil etc. They are not profit oriented and money minded in their trades. Generally their trade seems to focuss on the fulfillment of daily consumable goods and for the use of the leisure time. Some of the Rajbanshi families do have such a simple and limited trade as their main occupation. Most of the Rajbanshi's on an average do have less interest and self-confidence in their trade. In this way, the economic life of Rajbanshi's is not effected directly by their occupations.

(iii) Cattleing (Animal Farming)

The next economic source of Rajbanshi's is pet animals. But now-a-days because of deforestation and the pressure of population growth, all the fertile land has been cultivated. So, animal farming is becoming more and more difficult due to lack of grass and the grassland to graze. They compulsorily use to tame at least a couple of male buffaloes or bullocks. Besides they use to tame cows, Buffaloes, goats, duck, swans and pigeons etc. They use to tame pigeon, goat and duck only for worshipping (offering to the god) and for eating meat. Occassionally they use to sell them in the market. Except these animals, they use to tame cows and buffaloes for milk, curd and also for the production of bullocks and male buffaloes. They use to prefer meat more than milk and curd. So, they use to sell milk and curd in the market and buy fish and meat as well as other daily needs. Because of the lack of the land for grazing, they are being compelled to tame only two or three animals per house with the help of tethers and cords for fettering cows and buffaloes as well as 2 to 4 goats. They do have problem to add more. In this way, their source of income is simple and limited by means of pet animals too. Inspite of not being counted as a source of income directly, most of the Rajbanshi's tame dogs for guarding and protecting their houses and pet animals from thieves; jackals, marten and other wild animals.

(iv) Labour

In Rajbanshi community, labour is also a source of income. Some of the families in Rajbanshi community use to pass their lives being labourers lifelong. Their main source of income is labour. There is a tradition of division of labour according to (on the basis of) gender and age in Rajbanshi community. For example:

- *(a)* Work of children
- *(b)* Work of old people
- *(c)* Work of husbands/men
- *(d)* Work of women

(a) ***Work of children:*** The boys and girls under the age of 10 are being counted as children. If they are boys, they use to guard or look after the cows and other pet animals as well as help their families in the work of agriculture as much as they can. If they are girls, they use to help their mothers, elder sisters and sisters-in-law in simple household activities. In the spare or leisure time children go to the terraces of the fields and other places where they find water freezing for fishing and catching the crabs. In this way, the children in Rajbanshi community, use to help their households in daily behavioural activities from the very beginning of their age.

(b) ***Work of old people:*** Above 60 years, people are being counted as old ones in Rajbanshi community. Their activities are: caring the small children in the house, looking after the house etc. They use to make tethers, net for fishing as well as advising their family members in a behavioural term. In this way, also the old people in Rajbanshi community use to help others in their

family as much as they can.

(c) *Work of husband:* Here, in the sense of male, the young men or the capable men are being counted. The activities of these people are: ploughing the field, help in social work and facing the problems seen in their behavioural works. Rajbanshi young men are the main pillars in the economic life of Rajbanshi community.

(d) *Work of women:* The work of women in Rajbanshi community is: keeping the house neat and clean, preparing food, making rice and flour etc. for preparation of food etc. Besides these works, looking simply after their cows, prepare a variety of rice snacks as refreshment in the spare time and making rice using mortars, etc. They use to sell beaten-rice, Murahi (a variety of rice snacks) and vegetables in the local market. Women in Rajbanshi community are more active than men. The Rajbanshi women cannot help much in the agricultural work like in sowing seed, etc.

(v) Supplementary Income Sources

The supplementary Income sources in Rajbanshi community are: weaving (act of making cloth, knitting mats and oval cushion) and employment opportunity. They use to make bedsheets for covering their beds and knit mats with the mixture of jute and cotton made thread in line with their own necessities keeping looms in their houses. They do these work mostly to fulfill their household needs. The jute-mats and bedsheets made at the looms in their houses are rarely being carried and sold in the market by Rajbanshi families. All these works are be performed in simple conditions and at limited cost of production.

The next supplementary income sources being employment. In comparison to other castes of Nepal, the Rajbanshi's who are the inhabitants for many years are being ahead of this number. No Rajbanshi is being posted in the high government posts of Nepal. Inspite of being less in their number, Rajbanshi's are being found working as the officials of the Panchayat (Village Development Committee in these days) in their own local areas and being personnels as the non-gazetted staff of different posts like Bahidar, Mukhiya, Khardar etc. as well as being teachers in local schools. Rajbanshi's are not interested to make the office employment as their main profession. The main reason of being so is that they use to be hesitating in order to be adjusted in other communities leaving their own community. Consequently they are not being able to go to other places in search of employment except the employment opportunity being found nearby their homes.

(b) Expenditure

The expenditure is also one of the main part of the economic lives of Rajbanshi's. As much they earn, so much is their expenditure. Because of being more expensive by nature, Rajbanshi's are continuously heading towards poverty day-by-day. The expenditure includes all their behavioural needs and all other expenditure for the achievement of happiness and satisfaction like the feasts and festivals, different ceremonies, marriage feast and each and every problem solving activities, etc. Expenditure on food and cloth is most necessary whereas expenditure on different ceremonies, feasts and festivals, marriage etc. also should be assumed as necessary. But the groundless overexpenditure on these activities is being assumed as unnecessary. There is an established tradition found in Rajbanshi community of expending unnecessarily. They don't think about ranking their unlimited wants according to priority of the necessities. At the time of being unable to expend fully from their own property (savings) earned, they sell their pet animals like cows, bullocks, male buffaloes etc. If the money needed doesn't become enough they borrow or take debt from others, promising to pay a high rate of interest too and gradually they become unable to repay the debt. So, they are compelled to sell their land (field) at a cheap rate. In such a way, they don't be afraid of the expenditure to be done by themselves.

As a result, many of the Rajbanshi's who had owned 30/40 Bighas of land[1] 10/15 years ago are being the owners of 3/4 Bighas these days. Some of the families are already seen as having no house and land of their own in their country of origin. There is no any limitation on their expenditure. They are compelled to take loan from the moneylenders promising to pay with their agricultural products at a cheap rate before harvesting their crops. Their special expenditure takes place on their feasts and daily food. They eat fish and meat just after one or two meal. They have no any feelings about collecting the property (savings) being simple in their food and behaviour until having a little property with them.

Their main areas of expenditure (spendings) are as follows:

(i) The daily consumable goods like food, cloth, salt, oil, cigarette, meat etc.

(ii) Expenditure regarding agriculture like land tax, cultivating and harvesting cost, bullocks, male buffaloes, seed, labour, wage and irrigation channels etc.

(iii) The feasts and festivals including ceremonies, expenditure on wedding ceremony and worshipping etc.

(iv) Others like casual disasters, demise, hospitalities, treatment and schooling etc.

Among the expenditures mentioned above, the expenditure regarding agriculture is most necessary. Likewise, the expenditure to be done on daily consumable goods is most necessary but in their food they like fish, meat, oil and spices on which the amount of expenditure seems high. On marriage ceremonies, feasts and festivals they use to spend money unnecessarily. The different activities regarding marriage which continue upto one or two months, are most expensive because they use to buy fish, meat and other varieties of food as well spend a large amount of money on other formal hospitalities. Because of the fear of social criticism, some of

---

1. Bigha is a measure of land which is five-eighth of an acre.

the conscious young Rajbanshi's use to remain silent inspite of having all the good knowledge of it. Similarly, they are fond of singing and dancing, mondi's and fairs, feasts and festivals, etc. They are not being able to stop unnecessary customary expenditure in any condition in such an expensive age having limited earnings of them. The most expensive different varieties of food are compulsorily needed in each and every feasts and festival ceremonies, marriage feast and other customs of them. They also feed fish and meat compulsorily in death-feasts too. On a simple death-feast an amount of Rs. 1000 to Rs. 1200 is to be managed, whereas the expenditure cannot be accounted well regarding wedding and other ceremonies including feasts and festivals.

Summing up, the different things mentioned above from the micro angle, we can confine that the economic lives of most of the Rajbanshi's, except some of their families, is being passed in a great trouble and poverty according to comparative study made between their income sources and expenditure, including their daily behaviour, manners, settlements, customs and hospitalities etc.

V

Festivals

(PAWANI)

Festivals are being called "Pawani" by Rajbanshi's. They are fond of Pawani's, fairs, feasts, singing and dancing. Rajbanshi's celebrate different Pawani's for merry-making, recreation, enjoyment and for their welfare including happiness and satisfaction. Dashain and Tihar; as they are being celebrated by the Hindus of Nepal, are also being celebrated by them. During the course of celebrating Dashain, they worship goddess Durga with the offerings of uncastrated he-goats, pigeons, Swans etc. on the eighth and ninth days, but they don't have the culture of having Tika and Jamara (young shoots of barley cut at Dashain). Likewise, they use to worship the goddess Laxmi in their own way during Tihar. But they don't have the custom of Bhai Tika (having Tika from sisters). Each and every Pawani of Rajbanshi community do have their own cultural and social importance as well as their own distinctive characteristics and stories.

The main Pawani's of them are as follows:

(i) Dol-Siruwa:

The main Pawani of Rajbanshi's is Dol-Siruwa as Dashain festival of Brahmins and Chhetries. Rajbanshi's celebrate

Dol-Siruwa with great interest and as entertainment. Dol-Siruwa starts from 2nd Falgun (February) and ends at the 2nd day of Baisakh (April) the new year. Dol or Siruwa are the names of the same Pawani. The time period between the Falgun-Purnima and the last day of the month Chaitra is called Dol and afterwards upto the 2nd day of the month of Baisakh is called Siruwa.

(ii) Dol-Pawani:

The Pawani which comes in existence on the full moon day in the month of Falgun (February/March) is Dol-Pawani in Rajbanshi community. It starts since the fourteenth day (chaturdasi) of the bright half of the lunar month Falgun (Feb./March) and ends on the third day called pratipada of the dark half of the lunar fortnight. They use to say 'Bhailaghar' to the fourteenth day mentioned above. 'Bhailaghar' means to bury a bamboo in the rice field or dry field tying some hay in it. In this festival, Rajbanshi's use to smear their houses and courtyard as well as wash their clothes on that day. On this occassion, Rajbanshi villages are to be seen as new places of attraction. After establishing the 'Bhailaghar' they go there and worship by using Adhikari (the Rajbanshi priest). At this time, it is found that the Kirtiniyas use to sing hymns. After the completion of all these activities, the promise makers use to lit a fire in the 'Bhailaghar'.

On the full moon day, next to Bhailaghar, the act of smearing the house and courtyard begins from easly in the morning. Having the belief that the Dol Thakur uses to come to their houses on that day, Rajbanshi's use to offer a kind of dry food prepared with rice flour called 'Puwa' worshipping with flower, incense and red powder etc. Dol Thakur is being assumed as their god in Rajbanshi community. It will be discussed in detail later. For the purpose of completing their promises, all the fire litters in 'Bhailaghar' use to manage a whole night hymn singing programme in their houses using the Kirtiniyas. Youths of Rajbanshi villages use to pass the whole night singing different songs regarding the praise of Dol Thakur. On the next day or the last day of the full moon day having month Falgun Rajbanshi's use to enjoy singing about Dol Thakur and play with some colour and red powder etc.

(iii) Bhedekhaili Tistabudhi:

After the end of Dol-Pawani, on the first day of the dark half of the lunar month Falgun, Siruwa Pawani starts since the first day of the new year. Bhedekhaili-Tistabudhi links and establishes the relation between Dol Pawani and Siruwa Pawani. According to the customary assertion of the Rajbanshi community, Dol Thakur uses to burn houses being mad because of having the poisonous white thornapple and intoxicating hemp on the 14th day of the bright half of the lunar month Falgun (March). This is the sense of burning the Bhelaghar on this day. The appearance of Thakur seems too dangerous on that day. The Thakur staggers hither and thither in his senselessness. Seeing the extraordinary occurrence and dangerous appearance of Dol Thakur, Thakurani (wife of Dol Thakur) comes out of sight of him being out of their house. Next to this day on the full moon day of Falgun, Dol Thakur comes to the house peacefully but doesn't meet Thakurani. He looks for her all around, inside and outside the house but does not meet her. So he goes out of his house in search of Thakurani. Just after it, Thakurani arrives at her house. She doesn't meet Thakur at that time. So, she also leaves her house in order to look for Thakur being much effected by his love. Both the Dol Thakur and Thakurani are believed as the god and goddess respectively in Rajbanshi community. Thakur and Thakurani seek for each other being bereft of as far as possible. But their appointment takes place on the bank of the river on the 2nd day of Baisakh which day is called "Ghatausari". This comes within Siruwa Pawani.

Bhedekhaili means the friends of Tistabudhi, who visit village to village. Tistabudhi refers to the artificial appearance of Thakurani while looking for Thakur. The tradition of following the Tistabudhi culture is being found in some of the Rajbanshi families. The followers of such an incarnation of Thakurani invite the villagers to take part in the procession accompanied with the singing of the Bhedekhaili songs. Only women use to participate in Bhedekhaili which starts since the eighth day of the full moon day of Falgun. On the first day of Bhedekhaili, they worship goddess Tistabudhi. They cover half of the Saji with a piece of white cloth and keep some rice in it where they burn a small earthen lamp and establish the image or the symbol of Thakurani. Saji is a flower-basket made with cane. Only the Masyani (Maryani) lift and carry that Saji using an umbrella. Maryani, with her Saji goes forward and Kaishalies use to follow her while singing. In this way they visit village after village. The women who carries the Saji (the representative of Thakurani) and leads others is called Maryani (Masyani). Similarly, the Rajbanshi young girls who follow Maryani singing songs in Bhedekhaili are called Kaishalies. The Bhedekhaili group sings a song regarding the search for Thakur first in each and every house which they visit. After singing this song they sing other different songs. There is a tradition of providing a warm hospitality to them in each of the Rajbanshi house together with presenting some rice and money including the worship to the Thakurani Tistabudhi established in the Saji. In the songs being sung on the occassion in Bhedekhaili by Kaishalies, Dol Thakur and Thakurani are assumed as lovers of each other. They sing more songs adversary to Dol Thakur together with satires to the young boys. Sometimes such a provocation becomes obscene too. Bhedekhaili is being called towards west whereas towards east (Jhapa) it's called Tistabudhi. Because of the worship of water being compulsory, they use to worship at the well or river.

A piece of song which is being sung while provocating the young boys in Bhedekhaili by Kaishalies is as follows:

Uttar dakshin dharata	In the houses of north and south
Aure Sakhi Lera re Chhahanire hai	Oh friend, the roof of hay
Dinera Savanga Bangla	The day's appearance; building (house)
Aure Sathi Rate Chuhe Panire hai	Oh friend, water leaks at night

Bhogi balar saija	the bed of wife owner
Aure Sakhi alincha do linchare hai	Oh friend, the bed of salaincha
Jalam dena ra seja	the bed of unmarried at all
Aure Sakhi dhansuka dhakarare hai	Oh friend, bamboo-mat for drying rice
Bhogiwala Sute	wife owner sleeps
Aure Sakhi hansite Khelite re hai	Oh friend, smiling and playing
Jalam thena sute	the very unmarried sleeps
Aure Sakhi Kandite mabite re hai	Oh friend, thinking and feeling
Bhogiwala uthe	wife owner gets up (in morning)
Aure sakhi hansite nachite hai	Oh friend, smiling and dancing
Jalam thena uthe	the very unmarried gets up
Aure Sakhi Kandite Bhabite re hai	Oh friend, weeping and feeling

The main message of Bhedekhaili songs is the separation of Thakur and Thakurani. The sufferings of being separated are sung by the Kaishalies in their songs as their free expressions. The suffering of separation is being symbolized in the song mentioned above which indicates the suffering about lack of meeting each other. Regarding this context a model song is as follows:

Khopate peruwa re nahi-nahi	There is no any pigeon in the wallet
Sakhi mor bade bakum bakum Bakum	My friend speaks: Bakum
Tora Sangai Pirati re nahi	I don't love you (no love)
Amer gachhata Amere nahi-nahi	there is no any mango on the mango tree
Sakhi mor malo keni jhata	why do you strike with a stick
Tora Sangai pirati re nahi	I don't love you (not love)
Penjarite Suga re nahi-nahi	There is no parrot in the cage
Sakhi mor bole Radha Krishna	My friend speaks, Radha Krishna
Tora Sangai Pirati nahi	I don't love you (no love)

Kalate chhailo re nahi-nahi	There is no 1baby in the lap
Sakhi mor kande kuhan kuhan	My friend weeps: Kuhan Kuhan
Tora sangai Piratire nahi	I don't love you (no love)
Kalasite jal re nahi-nahi	There is no water in the small pitcher
Sakhi more kare chhalkat chhalkat	My friend tosses: chhalak chhalak
Tor sangai Pirati re nahi	I don't love you (no love)
Nindate sapan re nahi-nahi	There is no any dream in asleep
Sakhi mor dule deshantar	My friend wanders: country to country
Tor Sangai Pirati re nahi	I don't love you (no love)

While walking in the villages singing songs at Bhedekhaili, they use to collect the presents given by the villagers. All the presents are to be spent on the necessary worship of Thakurani and on the feast for Kaishalies on the Ghatosari day (the 2nd day of the month Baisakh). The details about Ghatosari will be given in the following pages.

(iv) Siruwa Pawani:

Rajbanshi's enjoy celebrating Siruwa Pawani for great entertainment and merry making. This festival takes place from the 1st day of Baisakh to the third of it. Such a 3 day Siruwa Panwani contains different customary Siruwas in it. There is a tradition of preparing curry of seven kinds. Mixing this sort of curry with stale rice, they have it on the first day of Baisakh. Also there is a tradition of sifting and hanging the onion and garlic. It is Bisawa Siruwa on the first day of Baisakh, Rang Siruwa on the second and Kad Siruwa on the third day of the same month. In this festival of Siruwa Pawani, Rajbanshi's smear and decorate their houses and wash and clean their clothes and dresses. On this occassion of Pawani they prepare different special varieties of food like fish, meat, curd and beaten rice, gangi muri (curry made of Murahi and gram) and puwa (cooked and fried rice flour). They celebrate Pawani interestingly selling their household property, fields etc. if they need.

(v) Bisawa Siruwa:

The Siruwa Pawani is celebrated on the first day of new year (Baisakh 1st every year). On the Bisawa Siruwa day, all the Rajbanshi's, youngest to the eldest ones, enjoy splashing and pouring water on each other from the morning. All the men and women, youths and children take part willingly and happily in it. Sprinking and splashing the water on each other takes place upto evening continuously. There is a customary assertion that the rainfall is to be sufficient all over the year and the crops, pet animals as well as people do have happiness, satisfaction (welfare) if they play splashing water on the first day of the new year. On the Bisawa Siruwa day, all the Rajbanshi's smear and make sacred their houses and worship their own gods and goddesses. There is a tradition of hanging garlic and onion in each and every house for the protection from different diseases all over the year. The next meaning or rationale of hanging the garlic and onion is last year's toxin and diseases avoiding activity. From this toxin (Bish) Bishuwa or as a Pawani of avoiding toxin. Bishuwa Siruwa in Rajbanshi community has been taking place traditionally. In Rajbanshi Society there is the most popular custom of eating Seven Sagi (preparing 7 curries in a same pan atonce) on the Bisawa day and keeping the stale rice of night time having Panta Bhat with Seven Sagi on the next day.

(vi) Ranga Siruwa:

Ranga Siruwa takes place on the second day of Baisakh. There is a customary assertion in Rajbanshi community that the tradition of Ranga Siruwa is being followed for making the mother earth coloured with great joy on the auspicious initiation of new year. Also on this day as on the day of Bisawa Siruwa, they smear their houses, courtyards and clean their clothes and dresses together with the custom of worshipping their own gods and goddesses. On this Ranga Siruwa day, all the men, women and children of Rajbanshi community seem as sunk in red-powder and colour. In the evening, Rajbanshi old people, youths and girls go to the nearby river of their village and celebrate Ghatosari singing different songs and also do worship. They do have a belief of meeting the Dol Thakur and Thakurani on the bank of the river at this moment. Ghatosari is the last day of Bhedekhaili system. Women who come to celebrate Ghatosari, have a bath in the river and worship Dol Thakur and Thakurani. Then they drink water sinking an umbrella in the water of the river. After the completion of all these activities the things brought by them like gram, Murai, ginger, curd, beaten rice etc. as the offerings to Thakur and Thakurani, they exchange with each other. They celebrate Ghatosari on the river singing interesting songs as their great enjoyment. On that day, while returning back from the river, they bring some sand of the river and sprinkle it on their roofs.

(vii) Kad Siruwa:

The last day of Siruwa Pawani is called Kad Siruwa. This festival has been celebrated on the third day of new year (3rd of Baisakh). During the time of the arrival of new year, worshipping the earth, to be united with the earth, Rajbanshi community uses to celebrate Kad Siruwa. All the Rajbanshi's of different age in their community enjoy playing mud on that day. The scene of splashing the mud by the young boys and girls on each other seems so attractive. At this time, there seems no shyness in them. The scene of catching, chasing, fencing and pouring mud on each other seems more interesting.

On the above basis, we can confine that Dol Siruwa Pawani is the last Pawani of the year in Rajbanshi custom as well as the first Pawani of the new year too. In this way, Dol Siruwa; linking both the new and last year use to make its own existence and importance praisable in Rajbanshi's lives and communities.

(viii) Asari Ghasari:

Asari Ghasari worshipping takes place in Rajbanshi community on the choosed or fixed good day of the month Asar (June). On this day different families of the village gather and worship Indra and pray for a good and sufficient rainfall.

The main characteristic of this worshipping is the more use of fruits, curd, milk etc.

(ix) Dadhi Kad:

Most of the Rajbanshi's celebrate this festival making a promise to offer something or worship a diety after the fulfillment of their desire, whereas others use to follow their traditional culture. This festival is celebrated on the eighth day of the dark half of the lunar fortnight which takes place in the month of Bhadra. On this occassion the statue of Krishna is established and worshipped with the songs of praise extremely. Adding some water in the soil, the mud is made in front of the statue of Krishna and people are invited to play the mud. After the completion of worshipping activity, a raw coconut and a pumpkin like thing called 'Kuvindo' is kept. This game is started by the little boys first and the coconut snatching game is played by the matured Rajbanshi's later. In the course of snatching the coconut, one who wins and offers the coconut in the temple, is prized. The prize contains a loin-cloth and some rupees according to their capacity. Similarly, they rub some oil on a bamboo and tie some rupees at the top (tip) of it and bury some part of it from one side. A game is played using those things alike. One who climbs up to the top of the bamboo, wins the rupees tied on it. In this way the game is played and ends. The organizer of these games himself invites others to participate in the feast at his house in the evening.

(x) Jatra (worshipping goddess):

Jatra means 'Dashain'. There is no any custom of having Tika in Dashain in Rajbanshi community. In this festival, they greet the ninth day of a lunar month as the great worshipping day. On that day, each and every family worships goddess Durga offering a Dali (a cluster or bunch) of bananas. They put a bunch of bananas on the claymade plate and betel on it. On that betel they put a betelnut too. If they do have the earlier promise to offer something, the tradition of offering uncastrated he-goats and pigeons takes place. On the ninth day of the lunar month, all the Rajbanshi Ojhas purify their all vedic texts or hymns in the temples of goddess Durga. On the first nine days of the bright half of Ashwin (Sept./Oct.), they purify all their tools and equipments with Gadnar (red and white clay). On the tenth day of a lunar fortnight, all the Rajbanshi's try be at the fair, wearing new dresses and having their food. The fair takes place in any Durga Temple. The fair market of that day is being called Kani Bazar and Nasia Bazar too. The Rajbanshi's of Jhapa go to the Durga temple at Garamuni and the Rajbanshi's of India, decorating their bullock carts together with their families go to Ghantola of Purnia district.

(xi) Lakhi Puja:

According to the Hindu tradition, Rajbanshi's celebrate Tihar as Lakhi Puja. Lakhi Puja means Laxmi Puja (worship of goddess Laxmi). This festival takes place on the day of the new moon in Kartik month. The worshipping activity starts from the day of the new moon and remains up to the coming of full moon day containing simple entertainments in Rajbanshi society. In this community, the main worshipping days of this festival are: *(a)* the day of the new moon, and *(b)* the first and second day of the lunar fortnight which are called Hakahaki, Bakhar and Tapa respectively.

Hakahaki: This day is the day of worshipping goddess Laxmi by all the Hindus. Rajbanshi's name this day as Hakahaki. Hakahaki is a special kind of sheet or tongue of flame from dry jute sticks. From early in the morning on this day, they make the cows taming place neat and clean including smearing the houses, courtyards and also decorating the houses with different coloured papers. In the evening, they worship cows using things like some paddy in a new winnowing fan, some water in a water-pot, the leaf of a betel, swan egg, red powder, an earthen lamp etc., tools for worshipping. After the completion of the worshipping activity, they make their houses, courtyards, wells all around resplendent, burning earthen lamps and candles. After burning the lamps in and outside their houses, Rajbanshi's rush towards their croplands making the sheet or tongue of flame with dry jute sticks to play Hakahaki. After reaching their croplands, all of them utter the Hakahaki sounds as in the examples given below:

Hakale Hukile (Hakkalire Hakkulire) dado dadi alole
Hansera dima kachur phuti aege mahalakhi hamara biti soro soro paka bhakara dura pala
Ae mahalakhi ghara Sandhya.

The main message of this stanza is as follows:

1. The motive of showing the light to their forefathers.
2. The intention of eulogy praise of Mahalaxmi.
3. This day is the day of worshipping the egg of Swan (duck) and having the curry of arum which are the favourite things of Mahalaxmi. So, it is the motive of motivating (calling) Mahalaxmi towards ourselves.
4. The intention of total destruction of insects and grasshoppers and intention of making our houses the resting place of Mahalaxmi (the goddess of wealth) clear and clean.

On that day, specially in their food (dinner), they have the arum vegetable (leaf of arum) and rice as the food offered to an idol together with the pulse of arum. No garlic, chilly and turmeric are allowed to be added in that days rice or the pulse of arum. The earlier promisers do a kind of worship named 'Gariguri' on this day. There is a custom of sacrificing ducks and uncastrated he-goats in this worship. In the house where the Gariguri worship takes place, they entertain the whole night with songs and dances.

Bakhar: Bakhar takes place next to the day of the new moon. There is a tradition of feeding Bakhar to their cattle. That is why this day is called 'Bakhar'. Bakhar means the mixture of a kind of tree called Tari, Salt, leaf of Dulphi (vingaraj) and Kalkeshariya which is for feeding the cattle. On the same day, Gariyan Puja also takes place according to the tradition in Rajbanshi society. Gariyan Puja means the worship of Gobardhan (the idol made of cow-dung). There is a concept of 'A good crop of tea where vingaraj grows'.

While at the worship of Gariyan, Rajbanshi's make three dolls of cow-dung and worship them with the egg of a duck, milk, banana and vermillion. The worshipping material is kept in the places of cattle at night. The earthen lamps are burnt both inside and outside their houses on this day too.

Tapa: The next day to Bakhar is celebrated as Tapa. On this day or previous to it, the idols established for different purposes as their gods and goddesses and worshipping materials are thrown in a sacred place like public road etc. From the point of view of worshipping, Tapa uses to be assumed as the last day of Tihar although from Laxmi Puja to the full moon day of the lunar night to come, Rajbanshi society celebrate Tihar with different songs and dances.

Hudhurdhura (Hudhul): It is a common culture of Rajbanshi's. This is one of the traditional customs of Rajbanshi society which takes place on the auspicious ceremony of the festival, Tihar. As Deusi, Bhailo is played in the society of the hilly people, the Rajbanshi children of 14/15 years sing Hudhurdhura in their community.

(xii) Bhaktiyar System:

Some people from Rajbanshi community worship Bhaktiyar. This is a kind of expensive worship. This worship is being used for having more strength. In Bhaktiyar, God Shiva and Goddess Kali are worshipped. Inspite of not being compulsory to worship Bhaktiyar by all the Rajbanshi's whose ancestors had followed this tradition, they worship Bhaktiyar on the auspicious ceremony of their first son's birth or after the completion of their sons' wedding ceremony. If they don't have son, they use to follow this custom after the marriage of their daughters or at least once compulsorily in their life time. According to the Rajbanshi's, the Bhaktiyar Puja (worship) is equal to the worship of Bhadrakali done by Ravan underground as narrated in Ramayan. In this worship, all the responsibility is of Debanshi who is the main enchanter of Bhaktiyar Puja. He conjugates some persons through the effect of his own hymns. The person who is conjugated by Debanshi, is called as Bhaktiyar. In the initial period of Bhaktiyar Puja, a man with the mask, assuming like an image of Kali (goddess), is followed by a group of Rajbanshi's who visit village to village for begging. This custom takes place upto seven days continuously. Begging is merely a custom of them. There is also a tradition of playing bands called Dhak Baja (a kind of drum like band) during the course of begging. On the last day, the statue (image) of Kali and the followers' group use to visit the market too. In the evening of that day, worshipping takes place in the houses of those Rajbanshi's who use to worship Bhaktiyar.

At first, while worshipping a Gamira Ghar (hut) is made. Gamira house refers to the hut made for worshipping Kali (goddess) secretly. All the worshipping activities are done in this house. The main religious treater of Bhaktiyar (Debanshi) worships secretly. All the open place outside the Gamira house, establishing a wooden piller and an instrument like thing is made for winding the veneration. This seems like playing instrument of children which sounds and makes as Chakachuli. But such an event that is arranged here; is the starting of rounding Bhaktiyar while pulling the rope from downwards. In the previous night of Bhaktiyar worship, Debanshi conjugates one person using hymns. The person conjugated by the effect of hymns becomes fully empowered. He brings a banana tree and a bamboo uprooting himself. The banana tree is planted (burried) in front of the Gamira house. There is a tradition of dramatizing a drama based on the story of Boat-man and Boat-woman at that night. In the story of that drama, the scenes of the birth of boat-men son and the boat-woman carrying food to the plough-man are shown. On this occasion, Rajbanshi's sing different satiric songs about the social disasters. Debanshi utters the hymns heading towards the same person who had been conjugated and mutter the Bhaktiyar rounding house as the muttering of a conjurer. The house owner excuses with the mutterer about his mistakes and prays for the fulfillment of his works. In this way, this night ends compleing the things to be done mentioned above.

The next day, Debanshi worships the Bhaktiyar rounding pillar in the open place in front of Gamira-house. Then

Debanshi worships inside the Gamira-house. At this time, the house owner fulfills the demands of Bhaktiyar rounding person and makes him happy. After this, there in Gamira-house, a pit representing the funeral pyre is made in which Bhaktiyar rounding person is made sleep keeping his head on the foot of the house owner as like as a corpse and as for symbolizing the shroud, a piece of white cloth is used for covering that person's body. Then they worship over the white cloth. After the end of worship, Debanshi thrusts the iron-fork in his backbone. Because of the effect of the hymn of Debanshi, the iron-fork doesn't cause any trouble. Inspite of the iron-fork being thrust entirely the person is called Bhaktiyar. On the other side, decorating and ornamenting Kali, the act of rounding the Gamir-house up to 5 times takes place. At the end of rounding, the representer of Kali cuts the banana-tree in only one strike which had been planted in front of the house last day. Just after the completion of these activities the image (representative) of Kali goes 5 times around the piller established for rounding Bhaktiyar and the mask of Kali is opened. Hanging the mask on the pillar Debanshi worship it. After it, Bhaktiyar is brought there and the iron-fork thrust in his backbone and the rope tied in the waist, uses to be tied lying flat upon the face in the large beam joined with the pillar and made round. The time for rounding is not fixed. While rounding the Bhaktiyar, the Dhak-Band players also use to be around the pillar together with their band playing and spitting, having and grinding Murahi and banana. At the place for rounding Bhaktiyar, crowd of people seems like a fair.

There is no compulsion of being Rajbanshi for rounding Bhaktiyar. The position of Bhaktiyar system in Rajbanshi community is assumed as a kind of duplication because the person for rounding the Bhaktiyar, before going to the Bhaktiyar (although his ancestors may be alive), the offering of food and water to his ancestors may have been done by Debanshi. In Rajbanshi community the Bhaktiyar is called almost dead because of the fork being thrust in his back and sacrificed to Goddess Kali. No one wants to be Bhaktiyar.

Therefore, Debanshi makes someone compelled by the medium of his hymns and conjugation.

In Rajbanshi community the position of Bhaktiyar and Danguwa seems as the same. As the Danguwa belonged to his wife, Bhaktiyar is under the control of Kali because of being sacrified to her. Both of them don't have worshipping and obsequal rites in honour of deceased ancestors. They and their families are always perceived by the society ranking them in the lowest grade.

Now-a-days this tradition of Bhaktiyar Puja doesn't exist, except at few places of Jhapa district like Ghailaduwa Village Development Committee's, some of the Rajbanshi families and some other places. The possibility of this worship being vanished from Rajbanshi community is its over expensiveness. The estimate of the budget needed for this worship is between Rs. 1500 to Rs. 2000. Now-a-days some of the conscious Rajbanshi's are starting to protest against Bhaktiyar system in their society.

(xiii) Jituwa (Chalachau) Pawani:

Among the different Pawani's which have been celebrated in Rajbanshi community, Jituwa Pawani is also one of them. As the Bhaktiyar Puja, Jituwa Pawani is also being celebrated by the Rajbanshi's in their community whose ancestors and families had celebrated traditionally. It is not compulsory to be celebrated by all. At the Jituwa celebrater clan or family this Pawani is being celebrated yearly or in the year of the marriage of the eldest or youngest son. If someone does not have son at that time, in the year of the daughter's marriage or at least once in their life time. Such a religious vow must have been done which is believed by Rajbanshi's. Inspite of this tradition not being followed generally, in some families they use to celebrate it only if they have promised earlier. Only the women use to be in fasting in Jituwa as on the day when women fast and pray (Tij) which is being celebrated by other castes of Nepal.

The fasting of Jituwa refers to the fasting of the King Jita. Indrajit; son of the King Ravan of Sri Lanka as described in

Ramayan, is being assumed as the King Jita in Rajbanshi society. This Pawani is also exactly alike with Bhaktiyar which takes place mostly in the month of Ashwin. From the dark half day of the lunar fortnight, the Rajbanshi women used to be in fasting. On the first day of their fasting, a square sized pond is to be made in the middle of the courtyard. The banks of the pond (Ghat) are to be made in all the four directions of the pond. On the land, at the middle of the pond Saja is kept. A flower, symbolizing the picture of King Jita is decorated in an earthen pot (Handi) which is called 'Saja'. Saja used to be covered from the upper side. A pair of living Magur fish using vermillion used to be made free from the eastern bank of the pond. Women in fasting use to stay towards the west. Around their seats there used to be decoration of many Delas (the betelnut kept on the bunch of banana). All the time incense and earthen lamp are burnt. Crowd of villagers gathers around the pond. Women in the first fasting of their life can have the diet of fruit only after distributing Delas to five persons on the first day. In their diet of fruit, salt and oil are restricted except meat and fish. The act of fasting and worshipping takes place upto 3 days in Jituwa. The main worshipping God at the time of Jituwa fasting is King Jita. Women used to be in fasting for the fulfillment of their own and their family intentions.

While hearing about the presence of Jituwa, groups of singers and dancers from different places use to the there. There is no need of invitation to them. Songs and dances of different types and places use to come up in the 3 days of Jituwa Pawani. First of all, the act of distributing Dela to the different groups of singers and dancers take place. There is a tradition of feeding them together with their hospitality. Among the songs and dances Chapan, Temki, Natuwa etc. are the main ones. Disguising the dress and appearances of jokers, dancers and singers come there. All these should be distributed Dela as the food offered to an idol by 'Marjyani'. Women fasting in Jituwa are called 'Marjyani'.

(xiv) Ananta Dora:

Ananta Dora which takes place in Bhadra (August/ September) is being celebrated as Pawani in Rajabanshi community. There is a customary assertion in Rajbanshi community about Ananta Dora which is based on the story described in Ramayan when Ram, Laxman and Sita went to the forest according to the order of their father. Laxman used to be in celibacy up to the whole period of 14 years. He did not look at the face of women in that period and only having the diet of fruits he had controlled himself. After the completion of the duration of 14 years, because of the effect of fasting a supernatural power was created in him which made him able to kill the brave Meghnath (Indrajit); the son of Ravan in the battle. They say that the custom of fasting has started from that time. Particularly this fasting is only for male ones but somewhere the women also participate in this fasting.

Persons who want to worship Ananta Dora should be in fasting from the first day of the Lunar fortnight of the bright half of the Lunar month Bhadra (August/September). People in fasting period are not allowed to have the rice (Bhat) or boiled rice. In this way, the days used to be passed up to the 13th lunar day of the bright half of the lunar month on which day they have Sajam. Sajam is a kind of food which contains rice pudding and fruits. Having Sajam means to have something only after seeing the stars in the sky in the evening after fasting all the day. On the next day (14th lunar day) they use to plant 4 banana trees in the 4 directions of the courtyard and also they plant one banana tree in the middle which seems like a fame. Together with each and every banana tree, a metallic vessel with a narrow neck (Kalash) is to be kept there with some water in it. Place for farming is smeared and made sacred. Then the priest (Terain priest) starts worship with different worshipping materials. Among the worshipping materials, 14 types of fruits and the bunch of banana having only fourteen pods is mainly needed. After the end of worship and hymn of praise, the priest ties some thread in the right arm of the fasters and gives some rice and flowers offered in worship to them and people who were in fasting (fasters), give some presents to the priest. In this way, the act of worshipping comes to an end.

In the beginning of the worship of Ananta Dora, after adding the fasting of 14 years, they must have the rules observed by Laxman, but such a rule is seldon followed. Rajbanshi's do have the concept of storing the strength in themselves following the 'Ananta Dora fasting' up to 14 years. After completing the 14 years of Ananta Dora fasting, there is no need of worshipping and fasting in the Rajbanshi's life.

Besides the different festivals mentioned above, Rajbanshi's celebrate Magh Sankranti (the first day of the month Magh), the eleventh day in a lunar fortnight etc. too in their society.

VI

Religious Belief

All the different castes and communities do have their own traditional systems, religions, festivals and ceremonies including fundamental religious belief. They do have their own traditional belief in gods and also the worshipping process of them. In this way, for the entertainment in their life and for religious service, they enjoy singing, dancing, adoration etc. All these customs are traditionally accepted by their society which is the culture of that caste. Here, we have to discuss the culture of Rajbanshi caste.

Rajbanshi's are the living caste owners having their own existence from the very beginning. These things are clearly stated in their castewise history. Rajbanshi's do have their own language, counterfeit dress, living style, society and culture. Thus Rajbanshi caste can be accepted as a complete indigenous group of people having their own caste among others.

Rajbanshi's do have fixed faith in their religion. It is found that in Rajbanshi's religious services are accompanied in any way in their each and every festivals, ceremonies, worships and different cultural activities. Inspite of having Hindu religious duties, Rajbanshi's use to worship their own gods and goddesses of their fundamental belief which are not found in Hindu religion's sacred books, although Rajbanshi's worship them showing their relation with Hindu gods and goddesses. Inspite of being the followers of Hindu religion, their worshipping methods and traditions are different with others. There is no any difference found in the religious philosophy regarding this and the next world between Rajbanshi's and Hindus.

Rajbanshi's accept religion as kindness to others, be disciplined as stated in their traditional customs and not troubling others etc. Similarly, crime means telling lie, not being trustworthy, grabing others property, fornicating others wife, stealing, deceiving etc., activities which are out of social value and acceptance. Each and every method of thinking and contemplation seems effected by the religious trust of Rajbanshi's. For example, not having children, dying babies after getting birth, being sick and suffering from diseases, being poor, being rich and happy, getting enough child birth, dying untimely, being in accidents, wasting crops, lacking money and property, being stolen, being in burn, being rich and poor etc. all are being accepted as their luck and in accordance with the mercy of god. There are a great deal of religious superstitions found in them whereas they use to accept entirely the Hindu philosophy that the result of good things and crimes become available in this and the next world as well. The Hindu concept that the door of heaven will not be opened without having a son, is equally believed by the Rajbanshi's.

In religious terms, except different gods and goddesses, Rajbanshi's equally believe in ghosts too. Man died untimely or anyone who had lacked cremation and after the death of criminal person, there uses to be the presence of ghost which is their mass concept. They use to respect and worship ghosts to be protected from them. Worshipping ghosts entirely contains their fearfulness but not the real respect. In the religious books or in the customary assertions, there are stories about the supernatural strength of the gods and goddesses. In the same way, a lot of stories are found about the supernatural powers of ghosts. They do have a strong concept that no ghost or god and goddess use to trouble if we worship them.

According to the religious tendency (attitude), culture and methods of performing the activities of Rajbanshi's being perceived, the gods, goddesses and ghosts being worshipped by them, can be classified and studied as follows:

- *(a)* Gods and Goddesses of the house.
- *(b)* Gods and Goddesses of the village
- *(c)* Ghosts.

(a) Gods and Goddesses of the house:

It is found that each and every Rajbanshi establishes his family-god in the south-east direction from his house where the eldest person of the house used to worship with burnt perfume and earthen lamp, being pure and sacred after having a bathe. The other members of the house can use to do that in the absence of the house owner or main person. Besides this, they use to worship Basil, Durga Devi (goddess), Kali and Hanuman also as their house-gods. According to them, while worshipping these gods and goddesses, if someone makes a little bit of mistake, tyranny takes place in their house. Except these, there are some of the god and goddesses which have been worshipped daily from the turn of their ancestors too. They are not compulsorily worshipped by all although the family which has been worshipping continues to do so. They use to worship all the gods and goddesses including Hindu ones and related to them too as their house gods. There is difference only in the worshipping methods. Among the gods and goddesses of their house they almost use to establish the statue (idol like) of Kali and Durga and worship them whereas others use to worship in their symbolic figures or pictures.

(b) Gods and Goddesses of the village:

In order to be protected from diseases, malady and lack of rainfall etc. together with the expectation of the progress in health, crops, pet animals like cows, buffaloes, bullocks, male buffaloes and goats, etc., Rajbanshi's use to worship their village gods and goddesses. Such a worshipping is a group worship of a village. The village gods and goddesses used to be placed in separate places from their village. No any sort of dirt is allowed to be thrown around the temple. The village god worshipping is the worship of strength. While worshipping banana, milk, insence etc. together with the sacrifice of pigeon and uncastrated he-goats are offered. Dulahi Chandi, Sarvamangala and Bishahari are the different appearances and groups of Shakti-kali being used to be worshipped as village goddesses. These village gods and goddesses are placed in temples. At some places making a small hut using hay whereas barely under the tree in other places, village god is placed.

Besides home and village gods, Rajbanshi's do have many gods and goddesses. It is found that Rajbanshi's worship Burma Thakur as their fire-god, Pawan Thakur for protection from storm-wind (gale), Bishto Thakur for water, Basumati Thakurani for the elimination of famine and Mahakal Thakur as the god of hill and forest.

(c) Ghosts:

Rajbanshi's do have a great self-confidence in themselves. They accept and worship ghosts equal to gods. The pregnant woman must obey and follow the rules for the protection of the child from ghost-gods. No pregnant women is allowed to go outside at night. She is forbidden to go to the house of a dead one and also to have some edible things where the offering of water and food etc. to Brahmins in honour and benefit of manes takes place. Tuesday and Saturday are the days on which they are restricted to go outside. Similarly, they are forbidden to cross the river while during the period of pregnancy, no living creature should be killed, otherwise ghost-god troubles. Pregnant women used to keep a piece of iron, knife etc. with themselves in order to be protected from ghosts. In some places there is a tradition of erecting the mop or a net or trap of fishering for protection from ghosts. Some of the pregnant women call to make ojhas cast a spell and tie a piece of iron in their arms. If the pregnant woman feels trouble or pain before the full time for getting a child birth and if the pain is movable hither and thither inside the stomach, that is called *Poiri Pith* which is a kind of ghost. If it attacks, ojha must be called. In this way, the negative effect affects from the prenatal stage in Rajbanshi community. Such an effect is being found equally in each and every Rajbanshi in the conscious period of their life.

They do have a concept that the presence of ghosts seems if someone dies untimely or if no offering of food and water to manes is given. The soul of them changes into a ghost in such a dissatisfactory stage and live in the bush of bamboo, on Sebara tree and other places., It can enter easily inside the closed room and can attack the human being at any time. It sounds like a walk of a dog or cat or makes people frighten throwing a clay-clod before attacking the human being.

Man affected by ghost trembles and do not talk with others in good manner. Sometimes they smile over and sometimes are over afraid of. If these symtoms occur in any human being, they call ojha who diagnoses the cause of the disease taking some water in a pot. He looks for ghost over there and asks, "Who are you?" If he does not get answer from the ghost, he covers the man affected by the ghost with the net and ties him with a rope, and sprinkles some water casting a spell. Because of the effect of spell, the man stands up and cries, murmers, abuses the ojha but does not tell the truth. Ojha casts a spell and sprinkles more water on him, only then the ghost tells about him. Ojha continues to ask. The ghost replies the main causes of troubling the man by the medium of the ghost-affected man. Ojha allows him to go from that place. The ghost demands (begs) some edible things to have, a little curd and beaten rice and chur (cigarette) smokes. Then the man affected by the ghost falls down on the floor and becomes unconscious. In this stage, Rajbanshi's become confident about the ghost having gone. They make the man stand up slowly. The man knows nothing about the happenings at the time of ghost attack period according to himself while being recovered.

The ghosts *Pyatani* and *Poiri* are assumed as dangerous. The ghost that seems to have emerged from the died unmarried girl is named as *Poiri* and a pregnant woman's corpse changes into the ghost named as *Pyatani*. The symptoms of the effect of ghosts on the children are : *(a)* Different coloured diarrhoea, *(b)* absence of sucking the mothers breast, and *(c)* weakness etc. If they do not use to treat or avoid the ghost through the medium of Ojha, children can die. Such a disease is called Bahena. If an unmarried girl is attacked by it, she uses to dream like eating something, having sexual intercouse with a man, laughing and murmuring etc. whereas if an unmarried boy is attacked by it, he starts day dreaming, eating something and having a sexual intercourse with a woman etc. which is called *Chhalana*.

If the symptoms mentioned above are seen in any person that uses to be the symbol of attack by a *Pyatani* or *Poiri*, Ojha is needed at this time who pronounces, spells and sprinkles water from Jhola Pada, Oil from Telapada and ghee from Ghee Ghada. After doing so, if the patient does not run away or cry and shout, it is assumed that the ghost has not escaped yet. In such a condition they do Pakpuja (a kind of worship) which is a simple worship for warding off the ghosts etc.

A banana leaf is kept in the place smeared with cow-dung while at Pakpuja they put some vermillion and black Tika at about 5 to 7 places as well as some rice, sugar, banana, milk and a piece of white cloth on another banana-leaf. They tie a thread upto the patient placed from there. After these activities, ojha uses to sketch a picture of a woman with some vermillion and black Tika on an another banana-leaf. He makes a banana leaf-cup and a tool for sipping a little water from the palm of the hand by way of purification and pours some water in it. After completion of these things, ojha uses to ask for a cage with a pigeon in it. Then the ojha uses to cast a spell, sprinkles water on the pigeon, puts a pigeon feather rooting out from the pigeon in the place of vermillion-marks and casting spells holds both wings of that pigeon and moves up to the head and down to the feet in front of the body of the patient. Then he keeps the pigeon inside the cage again. After completion of these activities the ghost used to escape. The purpose of exorcing the ill man with the use of a pigeon is to make the ghost *Poiri* enter into the body of the pigeon leaving the patient.

They count five sisters of *Poiri* as following:

(a) Mul Poiri, *(b)* Sarago Poiri, *(c)* Buda Poiri, *(d)* Nun Poiri, and *(e)* Budhi Poiri.

Rajbanshi's assume crematorium (Masan) as equally dangerous as other ghosts. One day, while Kali (Goddess) was having a bath in the river, Dharma (the God) arrived there. Then they established a sexual relation with each other. Consequently, Masan took birth from such sexual relation according to their customary assertion which lives at a distance from mens' residence. It's animal and for coveynance is a horse (steed). The Masans are of 18 types which do have their own habitats. For example:

(a)	Badiya Masan	—	lives in the cluster of bamboo trees.
(b)	Chhuchiya Masan	—	lives in the toilets.
(c)	Bohita Masan	—	lives in the pillar of banana-tree.
(d)	Chalna Masan	—	lives on the ways and roads.
(e)	Kala Masan	—	lives in the cremation ground.
(f)	Kuhuliya Masan	—	It can live in any appearance.
(g)	Timila Masan	—	It lives in water.
(h)	Ghater Masan	—	It lives on the bank of the river.
(i)	Nangha Masan	—	It roams naked.
(j)	Bisuwa Masan	—	It troubles the whole human body.
(k)	Ubuya Masan	—	Makes men vomit.
(l)	Sukana Masan	—	Makes men lean and thin and kills too.
(m)	Ugiya Masan	—	It disguishes differently and makes human being frightened.
(n)	Dyamasa Masan	—	It supplies diseases to human beings which troubles them frequently.
(o)	Mula Masan	—	makes human beings lose the way like a mad person.
(p)	Naraha Masan's hair	—	It becomes bald which troubles human beings much.

(q) Gaili Masan — lives in ways, paths, roads and attacks ill lucked persons.

(r) Rakta Masan — makes people vomit or excrete blood, etc.

The need of ojha is felt when these Masans attack people. Ojha makes the patient sit on a wooden seat in front of him and casts spell taking some grains of mustard in his hand, together with the movement of that hand from head to the feet of the patient. Then, ojha puts the mustard in a bamboo-cylinder and closes the cylinder (makes lid) with some pieces of rags and throws it into the forest at a distance which causes relief.

The next ghost named Magar is more popular in Rajbanshi community. Magars are of two kinds: *(a)* Kanta Magar, and *(b)* Jati Magar.

Kanta Magar contains eye in its chest and does not have head. Jati Magar uses to be tall. Particularly these Magars perfer to live on the trees near the rivers or ponds. These Magars attack people at night. Specially they use to attack the new brides and bridegrooms. Therefore, Rajbanshi newly married couples do not walk alone at night and do not cross the river at night. If the state of mind becomes weak, Magar will attack immediately and standing at the road and disguising him/herself as a dog, cat, jack etc. they frighten people.

When a Magar attacks people, the following symptoms are to be seen:

(a) Eyes use to be red, *(b)* chest aches, *(c)* being deaf, *(d)* trying to escape from the house, and *(e)* chasing and hitting the person who comes in front of him.

Such a Magar-ghost use to call someone using exactly as the familiar person's sound or voice. If someone comes out without any doubt at night, it carries him/her in the nearby pond or river and makes that person sink. It does not call 3 times. So people must not be out from their houses at night until it calls up to 3 times.

If somebody walks in a lonely place or road at night and looks an image standing with entirely white cloth he/she must stop atonce. The image seen is the Magar-ghost. If the human being (person) returns back, the ghost chases. So, while at being encountered with Magar, people must go back (step backwards) staring at it slowly. If it is Kanta Magar, it uses to stand under the tree. The person encountered must step backwards gazing towards that ghosts' eyes in its chest. If it is not possible to do so, own urine must be sprinkled all over the body. Consequently, the ghost cannot be able to attack, while at the time of the attack of Magar ghost the matter of calling Ojha is restricted in front of the person been attacked. Ojha must be called secretly otherwise, the ghost tries to kill the person before the arrival of Ojha. It is also believed that all the disorders shall be all right after casting spells by an Ojha.

There is another ghost popular in Rajbanshi community. The steed of this ghost is a Swan. The symptoms of its attack are as follows:

(a) being mouth, eye and every part of body wreathed
(b) being hands and legs becoming smaller and dry day-by-day.

The treatment of these things be done by the Ojha who makes a boat of a banana-pillar and also asks for a piece of white cloth, vermillion, lamp, a bunch of bananas, five metal rupees (coins), a swan, a pigeon and a picture of Kali (the Goddess). Then the patient used to be carried towards the bank of the river together with this worshipping material and then made to sleep for the purpose of exorcism using the swan and pigeon. Then he used to make the boat flow in the river tying the Swan and pigeon with it.

Rajbanshi's do have equal belief about Gods and ghosts. They are greatly frightened of the ghosts. There is a traditional custom of wearing anklet in a leg of their children and also tying small lockets of some herbs in order to protect them from ghosts which is called Morchakharu in Rajbanshi community. Besides this, there is a tradition of keeping fish-teeth, tiger-teeth and blue stone with themselves for protection from the ghost attack.

VII

Songs, Dances and Dramas

Each tribe or the family in the world, does have its fundamental cultural features. Only then will they be proud of their caste or tribe entirely. Life is not merely for labour and struggle but it needs pleasure, entertainment and welfare which is universal. So is the case in Rajbanshi's of the far east Nepal (Jhapa). Rajbanshi's enjoy, entertain, merry make etc. with the use of their different kinds of songs and dances. In some of these dances there seems the vital role of songs, zero songs in some ones and the main role of music in them.

(a) Songs and dances:

Rajbanshi's, by nature, are fond of songs, dances and dramas. Inspite of being their pertaining to socio-economic condition degraded they are making attempts to maintain and preserve their culture as far as possible. They make teams of singers and dancers among themselves and play for entertainment specially on different festivals and ceremonies. Rajbanshi girls do not participate in such activities. In the condition of the need of female characters too men disguise as female ones participate in singing as well as dancing activities. The main reason of not taking part by the girls in singing, dancing and drama is the narrow and controvercial concept of their society. The songs and dances of Rajbanshi's seem to be as simple and based on their traditions. Among the songs of them, there are several folk-songs found. All the songs used by them represent their religious devotion as well as the blind sensation of love affairs and taking vows. Most of the songs, used together with dances are found sung in groups. Concord between the songs and the actions of the dancers is not found exact although the gestures given by the hands and legs in agreement with the songs seems good. But a kind of expectation of people while looking at the dance cannot entirely be fulfilled as it requires wiggling the hips in dancing, bending bodies over together with the active presentation of appropriate gestures used by the dancers, etc.

The main bands being used in singing and dancing are: Khol, Dhulki, Harmonium, flute, etc. In each and every singing and dancing activity, for the purpose of providing much entertainment to the audience, a management of joker takes place decorating with a mask, artifical hair and other dressings who make the audience laugh telling different jokes, playing strange and peculiar roles, etc.

(b) Drama:

Rajbanshi's use to celebrate feasts and festivals, singing and dancing with great enthusiasm. In the same way, there seems a traditional cultural custom of dramatization in Rajbanshi community. The main purpose of playing and making play in the drama is religious devotion as well as entertainment. So, the presentation of dramas in Rajbanshi community is not only for the matter of entertainment but it is also for the achievement of the goal of religion.

The main role of songs and music seems to be in the dramas of Rajbanshi's. Similarly, it is believed that the personality of the character (role played) according to the story and the stadium or the stage managed for dramatizing, decides the success and failure of the drama. Because of the participation of the males only, the role of females used to be played by them, being ornamented, dressed and disguised as female ones. There must be proper management of the characters in accordance with the events, dressings and materials etc. needed. After collecting the things needed, they use to make a stage for dramatization at a higher place. They use to cover the stage all around it and make a temporary roof over it for the protection from dew and simple rainfall. The different dramas which are being popular in Rajbanshi community can be studied dividing in two parts. They are:

(a) Social and traditional dramas
(b) Religious dramas.

(i) Social and Traditional Dramas

Sastari and Pachali dramas which are popular in Rajbanshi community are categorized in this type. Sastari is also called Dhol Sahena drama. In this Sastari drama, a recent event from their society is dramatized by them. For example, someone causes a girl to run away or if someone makes his own wife to others', those events use to be joined in a sequential order together in the drama and use to play roles on them. Besides, they use their social disorders as satires in the story of that drama. The frequent jokes made by the joker together with different roles played for making people laugh, adds to to the success of the drama.

The story matter of Pachali drama used to be based on the traditional stories. In such a drama, an eventual story about a king or a crown prince is added in which the king or crown prince is involved in love affairs with a beautiful girl and tragedy in the middle and comedy at last, are the main dramatizing matters. Besides, Pachali drama also contains the traditional subject matter like: a story about a thief or robber, land-lord, patriarch or others who are assumed as respectable ones and their bad deeds in the village. In this way they use to reflect the indigestible behaviours making them as the main string of the drama's story. All the dialogues of the drama are spoken in songs. The responsibility of conducting the drama is reserved in the resource person (announcer) who can change the song immediately in line with the need of that time. Similarly, he use to play a vital role in a symbolic way for playing the role of different characters.

(ii) Religious Dramas

Religious dramas which take place in Rajbanshi community are entirely effected by religous feelings and all the story matters use to be related to their religion. Specially, the subject matter of religious dramas is taken from Ramayan and Mahabharat. Among the main dramas based on the story of Ramayan Lanka Gaan, war between Ram and Ravan, Sita's choice and acceptance as her husband, a rape case of Sita, Lav Kush etc. are more popular. Also are the dramas based on the story of Mahabharat. Such kind of main stories, are made as the main subject matter of drama. Besides, they use to prefer demonstrating the roles of trustworthy King Harishchandra in their dramas. The conversation of the drama used to be in songs or poems. There used to be the the main role of announcers and jokers as in social and traditional dramas.

They prepare the materials for ornaments, dressings and others needed for both the types of dramas mostly from their own locally available materials. Only the most necessary things which they could not make themselves, were bought from the market.

They use to be more enthusiastic in dancing and singing as well as in dramatization. They play roles in dramas, songs and dances continuously up to a weekend without being tired at all. Rajbanshi community offers an appropriate warm hospitality to the groups of singers, dancers and role players in a drama. They do have a good social prestige in their community.

(iii) Folk Songs of Rajbanshi's

Rajbanshi's are seen rich in their cultural aspect from the point of view of folk literature and folk songs. The use of folk songs is found everywhere in the feasts, festivals and different kinds of other cultural programmes which use to take place in their life. It is found that the traditional concepts of their life used to be stated in most of the folk songs and tunes of them. Folk songs are produced by the common folk. Now-a-days many of the Rajbanshi's use to sing some Nepali songs and folk songs learnt by the medium of Radio, although they take interest in singing the songs in their own language and tunes. In the folk songs of Rajbanshi's, the entire expression is found about love, pain, sufferings and the pangs of separation. In some of the folksongs there are found sacred feelings about the nature whereas some of the folk songs do contain the love of sufferings and the pangs of separation which sound heart touching to the lisliners. It is also found that there uses to be the presence of jokes and satires regarding the social disorders and socially unaccepted behaviours in their folk songs. Some of the folk songs used to strike peoples' mind having pathos in them. Some of the songs for example are given below: Nurturing, supporting and bringing the daughter up from the conception period when she becomes young the family members from the paternal home of the daughter are compelled to say farewell establishing the relationship with an unfamiliar person. While saying farewell to the daughter, everyone uses to be in great sorrow. This very influentiality to a high degree uses to be included everywhere in the songs being sung on the occassion of marriage ceremony by the people from the side of bride in Rajbanshi society.

A sample (model) of that song is as follows:

Chhata Sena Pusnu beti ge	I nurtured you daughter, from the small age.
Dudh Bhat diya	giving rice and milk.
Aji Sena jachhan beti ge	Daughter, you are going from today.
Daruna Shoka diya	making us more anxious
Maera chhilan arun darun ge	your were arun darun (so lovely) of your mother
Bapera chhilan bhari	And a burden of father
Jabar Kal jachhan beti ge	while at departure you have to go daughter
Darun shoka diya	Making us more anxious
Thali ta limu dudha bhata ge	I used to take rice and milk in a dish
Jhari ta limu jala	And take water in a mug

Beti beti daka parure mui	Daughter! daughter! I use to be calling
Beti nai mora ghara	There is no daughter in my house
Jei dinale chhilan beti ge	Daughter, you were on which day
Bhat Bandhihya	Being a rice cook
Jabar kale jachhan beti ge	while at departure, you are going daughter
Nidarun hya	making us more anxious .

The sorrow of separation having songs is also equally sympathetic and easy in Rajbanshi folk songs. By means of the planned words, feeling and sweetness of the tune in the heritage of their folksongs they use to be seen rich. A sorrowful song, for an example is given below:

Pranera pakhila prane ra kunkhila
Basanta jaya yadariya!
Diba nishi mana kandeche
Tumaka lagiya
Ashadhera jhumera dale
Ais ais pranera pakhi bhramara khaye
Pranera Pakhire pranera kunkhila

Purport (Meaning): A fully young girl remembers her lover who lives at a distance after having a look at the black-bees which seems engaged to suck the juice in the new shoots of creeper and in flowers at the time of the arrival of spring season. Seeing such a black-bee roaming hither and thither in the flowers, she compares herself with the flower of spring season and compares her lover with the black bee having absence of desire or passions in herself. A flower bloomed in the spring of youth but there is no any consumption of it because of the absence of a black-bee. The young girl appears sad in the mid-spring of her youth period.

According to the traditional custom of Rajbanshi's, husband's younger brother and sister-in-law, younger sister-in-law and husband of elder sister, the maternal aunt and nephew in their relatives are found to be more intimate and closer than other relatives. It might be so because of not being compulsory to offer the heavy formality among themselves. There uses to be the presence of talking shamelessly using jokes without any limit of them. In the course of using jokes in humorous ways, there used to be the use of sexual matters mainly in a symbolic manner which will be clearer after the study of the following folksong.

There is a conversation stated between the maternal aunt and nephew in the folksong below:

Banajhara gelena re bhagina	Banjhar (maternal Uncle) went oh! nephew.
Oure bhagina gelena batai dur	Oh nephew, he has gone at a distance.
Tor bade Dhai panghaichu bhagina	I've frozen curd for you.
Khaya keni re ja	go after having it.
Nahi Khamu dahi ge mami	I don't have curd maternal aunt.
Mama ei maribe toka	Maternal uncle will hit you.
Tora mamaka manae dimu bhagina	Nephew! I'll cause to agree your uncle
Kukure khaya gela	The dog had eaten (telling)
Banjhara gelena re bhagina	Banjhara has gone, newphew.
Aure bhagina gelena katae dura	Oh nephew! he has gone at a distance.
Tora bade chhagala Kataichu bhagina	I've cut a he-goat nephew.
Khaya keni re ja	Go after having it.
Nahi khamu masu ge mami	I don't eat meat aunt.
Mama e mari be toka	Uncle will hit you.
Tora mamaka manae dimu bhagina	Nephew, I'll cause to agree your uncle.
Kukure khaya re gela	Telling the dog had eaten.
Banjhara gelena re bhagina	Banjhara has gone, nephew.
Aure bhagina gelena kataye dura	Oh nephew, he has gone at a distance.
Tora bade bichhina parichu bhagina	I've prepared your bed.

Sute keni re ja	Go after having a sleep.
Nahi Sutima bichhinae ge mami	I don't sleep in the bed aunt.
Mamae maribe toka	Uncle will hit you.
Tora mamaka maṇaye dimu bhagina	I'll cause to agree your uncle nephew.
Sutakeni Re ja	Go after having asleep.

In Rajbanshi folksongs there is not only love, sorrow, pathos and the feeling of entertainment included but all the activities of their society are represented. The people of eastern and western hillside of Nepal, while at the time of the marriage ceremony, used to be debated in Sanskrit and Nepali couplet or stanza between the people from the girl (bride's) side and the persons involved in the marriage procession from the side of the boy (bridegroom) in which they use to insult and brag about their greatness, prestige, ability and richness etc. to each other. They try to justify their boastful tellings in poetic language (couplet). Similarly, there is a traditional custom of using songs at marriage ceremony in Rajbanshi caste. While at the time of marriage ceremony, people from the side of bridegroom sing songs insulting the people of brides side using different hitches in their songs both in houses of bride and bridegroom. Similarly, vice versa is also pertaining. All the songs used on this occassion are the folk songs based on their public tradition and custom. It is obvious that expenditure on various things uses to be high. Regarding this very matter on the first day of marriage ceremony, girls from the side of bridegroom use to sing songs insulting the people on the side of bride's father. An example of such a song is given below:

Khansang becha taka lago lago	Rupees from selling the tobbaco
Aimor kalamandi Chhile bharatigo	had filled my purse
Alima dalima guchha	Alima dalima guchha
Sala baniyora beti go go	The daughter of the greedy man
Aimor Kalamadanikole suna go	Made my purse empty

Alima dalima guchha	Alima dalima guccha
Pata becha takala go go	Rupees from selling the jute
Aimor kalamadani chhile bharati go	had filled my purse
Alima dalima guchha	Alima dalima guchha
Sala haramjada ra beti ra ra	The daugher of the blackguard
Aimor kalamadani kole Suna go	made my purse be empty
Alima dalima guchha	Alima dalima guchha
Asu becha takala go go	Rupees from selling Asu paddy
Aimor kalamadani Chhile bharati go	had filled my purse
Alima dalima guchha	Alima dalima guchha
Sala haramjada ra baheni go go	By the younger sister of the blackguard
Aimor Kalamadani kole suna go	My purse was made empty
Alima dalima guchha	Alima dalima guchha
Begana becha takala go go	Rupees from selling brinjals
Aimor Kalamadani chhile bharati go	had filled my purse
Alima dalima guchha	Alima dalima guchha
Sala baniyare beti go go	By the bloody greedy's daughter
Aimor kalamadani Kole sunago	My purse became empty
Alima dalima guchha	Alima dalima guchha.

(c) Language:

The language used by the Rajbanshi's of Jhapa is called Rajbanshi language which is a language from Euro-Indian family. This language is like the local dialect being used as Bengali language of north Bengal especially being spoken in the Bengal State of India. Although there are some dissimilarities found in vocabularies which are more distinctive than others in Rajbanshi language. However, in the course of study Rajbanshi language falls entirely under the impression or effect of Bengali language. Rajbanshi's use both Devnagri and Bengali scripts.

Rajbanshi's do ignore short and long forms of the pronunciation of vowels in the words of their language. They use to speak or pronounce whatever they feel easy. The pronunciation of the vowel sound a/d/ mostly becomes short, e.g. Jala, Mana, Dhana, etc. It is found that at the end of the word 'verb' they use to pronounce using long form of the vowels, e.g. khachhi/khachhi/jachhi etc. Not only in language but in the pronunciation of words too Rajbanshi language copies with Bengali. For example:

(*a*) 'ऋ' is a vowel which is pronounced as /r/ in Bengali and Rajbanshi e.g. Rishi (ऋषी), Rin (ऋण)।

(*b*) 'य' /j/ is a consonant sound pronounced in the same way as /j/ both in Bengali and Rajbanshi languages e.g. जमुना (यमुना), जदि (यदि), धर्म जुधिष्ठिर (धर्म युधिष्ठिर) etc.।

(*c*) 'ण' is a consonant sound pronounced as /n/ e.g. गुन (गुण), मरन (मरण), शरन (शरण), शोषन (शोषण) etc.।

(*d*) 'ब' is a consonant pronounced as /b/ e.g. बसन्त (वसन्त), देबता (देवता) etc.।

(*e*) 'क्ष' is a consonant sound pronounced as /kkh/ e.g. जक्खु (चक्षु), परीक्खा (परीक्षा), शिक्खित (शिक्षित) etc.

In this way, there is no great difference found between Bengali and Rajbanshi language specially in the pronunciation of sounds, rules of grammar and in the nature of language.

Some of the models or examples of words of both these languages are given below:

Rajbanshi	Bengali	Nepali	English
Bhala	Bhalo	Ramro	Good
Mitha	Mishti	Mitho	Sweet
Kharaba	Kharaba	Kharaba	Bad
Hamar	Abhar	Hamro	Our
Akash	Akash	Akash	Sky

Rajbanshi	Bengali	Nepali	English
Jal	Jal	Pani	Water
Kharu	Churi	Chura	Bangle
Bhagina	Bhagina	Bhanij	Nephew
Bari	Bari	Gaun	Village
Ashwar	Ashwar	Aunu	como
Jabar	Jaibar	Janu	go
Mui	Ami	Ma	I
Darbaja	Kebar	Dhoka	Door
Naka	Naka	Naka	Nose
Kana	Kana	Kana	Ear
Hata	Hata	Hata	Hand
Peta	Peta	Peta	Stomach
Mukha	Mukha	Mukha	Mouth
Barsha	Brishti	Barsha	Rainfall
Bhauji	Bodi	Bhauju	Elder Sister-in-law
Chaula	Chaula	Chamal	Rice
Hal	Hal	Halo	Plough
Tel	Tel	Tel	Oil
Ai	ma	Ama	Mother
Ba	Baba	Ba, buba	Father
Dada	Dada	Daju	Elder brother

VIII

Educational Status

The educational status of the inhabitants from the very beginning of Jhapa (Dhimal, Satar, Danuwar, Meche etc.) seems about in zero level. In them, Rajbanshi's, among others are seen in a higher rank in their educational status. But while comparing with other hilly castes, who are settling in Jhapa, the educational status of Rajbanshi's does not found to be satisfactory.

The main causes of the presence of such differences are:

(*a*) Their own traditional beliefs and ignorance about them.

(*b*) Inspite of having more or less knowledge about the importance of education they do not think about it seriously.

(*c*) They are tension free person depending upon luck and fate.

They like traditional concepts about the future of their children. Whereas some of the Rajbanshi's take interest in the education although they have failed to provide appropriate family environment to make their children study properly. At present, in the Rajabanshi community, the number of students in Primary, Lower Secondary and Secondary schools is increasing continuously so that it can be confirmed that there seems an effective expectation of the possible more or less improvement in the educational status of this community. Educating girls in Rajbanshi community seems about zero in its degree. It has been clear that they have not realised the urgent need and importance of education because even today their daughters and girls are assigned to perform household duties and activities like preparing food, guarding the house etc. Because of the effect of other castes, slight changes have been seen in such traditional concepts of them. Inspite of being less in number, the Rajbanshi's who live near the town and market, have been sending their children to the schools of their village for some years. But such Rajbanshi's who live near the town or market are less in number in comparison to those who live in the villages. In this way, the education provided to the girls of Rajbanshi community is only elementary or basic, whereas education being provided to the boys is also not found satisfactory. While at having a comparative study in the present context, it is found that the educational status of primary level seems satisfactory whereas the number of lower secondary and secondary education achievers' seems too low. The number of higher education achievers can be counted on a man's fingers too.

The main area of my study is also the secondary school of Ghailadubba, Jhapa which is one among the old secondary schools of this district. This secondary school is situated at the place where the density of population of Rajbanshi community is high. The children of Rajbanshi's study in this secondary school. On the basis of the data taken from the survey of 20 families for the purpose of study in 2044 B.S., their educational status appears as follows:

Total population	111
Number of literates	25
Literacy per cent	22.52%
Number of higher education achievers	x
Male literate people	20
Number of female literates	5
Number of school going age (6 to 8 years) children	15

Number of boys who can go to school	5
Number of girls (6 yo 8 years) who can go to school	10
Number of adults who are able to go to school	5

The data mentioned above makes clear the educational status of Rajbanshi community.

According to the study of the data mentioned above, the educational status of this community is not found satisfactory although the number of school going Rajbanshi children for some years has been increasing year to year. Bearing this fact in mind, it can be hoped that the educational status of this community will be satisfactory in the near future because if we study only about the status of some of the past years it is found that the number of school going Rajbanshi children was about zero in some of the schools where the density of Rajbanshi population was found high. But, now-a-days there is a remarkable change in the situation.

IX

Conclusion

While studying about the Rajbanshi's of Jhapa, the study about the geographical features had already been completed. Other factors need to be studied.

Jhapa is a district which lies in the far-east of Nepal. This region is the best from the point of view of agriculture because of being totally sandy and fertile soil contained in Terai Region. This is the main gate of eastern Nepal regarding transportation. The greatest highway of the kingdom of Nepal, Mahendra highway, starts from the Kakarbitta Village Development Committee of Jhapa. The southern and eastern parts of Jhapa are joined with Bihar and Bengal States of India respectively. Jhapa seems also as the main gate of eastern hilly area of Nepal. Inspite of only some samples of industries being found in Jhapa now-a-days it can be said that the future of Jhapa is certainly bright from the point of view of industrialization in the near future. This fact is being symbolized and proved by the enthusiasm and conscious awareness found in the different castes having settled here after migrating from different places. It is found that people of other castes have more consciousness, education and other enthusiasm regarding awareness except the inhabitants of this place who had settled here from the very beginning. Bearing all these things and situations in mind, it is necessary to study about the Rajbanshi caste which has settled in Jhapa since many years.

Among the inhabitants of Jhapa from the very beginning, Rajbanshi's are in the front list in every aspect of their life in comparison to Dhimal, Satar, Meche, Tharu, Danuwar etc. Rajbanshi's are respected politically, socially and economically too. But in comparison to the inhabitants of that place like Brahmin, Kshetri, Newar, etc., they are backward in every aspect of life. Inspite of being interested in education, Rajbanshi's are backward because of various reasons. They are entirely covered by the net of their traditional concepts, beliefs and customs etc. In traditional activities like feasts, festivals, different cultural activities and other ceremonies there is dominance of conservative matters regarding meaningful castewise characteristics too. The greatest meaningfulness of each and every festival, cutural activities and ceremonies be accounted on the basis of the management of feasts. Rajbanshi's, in this very demanding and expensive context, are deteriorating their own economic status day-by-day in an attempt to preserving their traditional and social prestige. There is the necessity of change in every aspect of lives of simple, gentle and good charactered Rajbanshi caste. If they continue their traditional activities, customs and other conservative behaviour, they will certainly be degraded after a couple of years and they will disappear like other inhabitants from the very beginning: Dhimal, Satar, Meche etc.

From the study of the different aspects of Rajbanshi caste it was found that they are a simple, honest and self-dependent caste. On the basis of their physical appearance and body structure, they appear to belong to the family of Mangol Dravidian clan at a glance but they speak the language similar to Bengali which is in Euro-Indian family. Inspite of being their society male dominated, the Rajbanshi womens' status is high. Rajbanshi men use to be serious about their household activities. In the same way Rajbanshi women feel their responsibility about their family. The role of women in Rajbanshi community is entirely active. It is accepted in their society that women are responsible about marketing and internal management of their houses. The next prominent custom found in their community is widow-marriage which is accepted completely by their society.

Cultural Aspect:

The cultural aspect of Rajbanshi families which are backward in educational awareness and other skillful works, seems only at the village level. Inspite of being so, it is found that the culture, religious activities and language of all the Rajbanshi's of Jhapa is the same except only some negligible things. They are not backward as compared to other castes from the point of view of their culture and folksongs. There is some difference in the processes and methods of celebrating and performing different festivals and customs although the cultural and religious aspect of them copies with the system if Brahmin and Hindu religion. The different customs and systems do have their own fundamentality in some of the places. By nature they use to be more as followers and fond of Shakti Puja and Balipuja inspite of having religious belief in all kinds of Hindu gods. They accept the existence of the god Shiva, Goddess Parbati, Kali and different ghosts as their source of strength. They do not follow the practice and system of sacrifice and burnt offerings in wedding, other cultural activities and in some of the worship of Hindu Gods and Goddesses. Similarly, all the Rajbanshi's of Jhapa categorize themselves under Kashyap clan. The Gods and Goddesses and ghosts which are being worshipped by them for years are totally different from Hindu Gods, Goddesses and ghosts. While studying about these things, it can be said that Rajbanshi's were possibly Koch before becoming Rajbanshi caste on the basis of their physical structure and some of the customs of them. It also appears that they had changed themselves from Koch to Rajbanshi during the course of a long period. They are not being able to accept the Hindu religion deeply uptill now. If they were the followers of Hindu religion, they would have followed all the rules, regulations, processes and systems of Hindu religion alike. There is no provision of marriage between the persons of the same clan in Hindus but Rajbanshi's have come in the Hindu religion after so many years and also they have determined their clan after many years. So, they are compelled to violate the Brahmin religion or the feelings and disciplinary activities of Hindu religion to be followed by being married in the same clan. Similarly, the Gods and Goddesses, used to be the matter of worshipping. However, they follow the Hindu religion these days. They do have a deep trust and boundless belief in Hindu religion. Now-a-days, their self-confidence regarding Hindu religion is a characteristic of them.

Social Point

While studying Rajbanshi caste from the social point of view, it is found that they establish close relationship not only with their society in a group but also individually. Their society decides about the amount of expenditure and the type of feast to be managed at wedding, death etc. including other worships and ceremonies. All the persons obey the decision made by their society and traditional beliefs. They are compelled to perform the activities inspite of being unable economically. If it is beyond the capacity of an individual to perform those activities, he/she must borrow, mortgage the land, sell the pair of bullocks or other goods in order to solve the problem in front of him, otherwise he will be criticized socially and boycotted by their society too. Rajbanshi's are more conscious as regards preserving their social prestige. They always use to be greatly afraid of social criticism. Their main source of income is agriculture. There is no any possibility of fulfilling the unlimited wants using the limited income of them. In such a condition too, they do not prioritise their wants to be fulfilled. They try to fulfill all their needs without thinking about their future. They depend on their fate, luck or spiritual and customary assertions.

The permanent property of Rajbanshi's is their land only. The economic condition of them was not so bad till the last 10 years. In comparison to other caste's, people who migrated in that place, were simple, gentle, honest and uneducated. Consequently they became badly effected by other caste people and also became the victim of overconsciousness and cleverness of others. Because of having the habit of doing too little work and eating so sweet, the ownership of land of Rajbanshi's continued to be transferred to others gradually. The 25/30 five-eights of an acre land owner Rajbanshi's of before 8/10 years, are living depending upon one or two five-eights of an acre of land at present. Some of such landlords are compelled to survive at the subsistence level working on wage and physical labour too. In comparison to the Rajbanshi's of north Jhapa, the Rajbanshi's of south Jhapa own a great deal of land uptill now because no other caste's people entered there for the purpose of settling there. But they are being debtors equal to their land's value by borrowing from the money lenders. In this way, this community is being greatly effected by the increasing rate of entry of the outer caste's people

They do have a narrow concept and feeling in other communities except in their own. Inspite of having trust and belief of others as for formality, they are entirely faithful. Their cultural and other castewise aspects are limited in themselves. The cleverness of other castes' people is the matter of fright and cause of not being well adjusted to Rajbanshi's. Their own traditional concepts, feelings and uneducated status is also the matter of being separated with other caste people. The hilly castes' people of this very area can go everywhere and also can easily adjust with other caste people. They do have the capabilities of consciousness, cleverness and work according to the flow of time in their habit and nature. Rajbanshi's are more backward in comparison to them in each and every aspect.

According to the study of these different aspects, the main cause of Rajbanshi's being backward is lack of awareness. They are backward in the aspect of education because of being fond of eating, sitting and celebrating different ceremonies lavishly and in their own ways. Inspite of taking an interest, they cannot educate their children well due to various reasons. The education provided to the girls is about zero in comparison to the boys. Similarly, there are no good conditions for their survival because of their increasing population day-by-day. Inspite of not being innocent about family planning and treatment of patients in hospitals, hundreds of infants die every year because of lack of proper and sufficient care as well as needed support including nurture too. The main cause of it is their overbelief on the treatment of conjurers. They do not believe in doctor and hospitals as they do it to the conjurer which seems usual because of not getting the facility of medical treatment in their villages.

Mainly the problems mentioned above, which are being found in Rajbanshi society of present Jhapa, are not so complex ones. So, it can be confined and there is no doubt that the Rajbanshi's of Jhapa can certainly be self-dependent in many ways as a special caste if the problems of them are solved respectively in all the related fields.

Bibliography

NEPALI

1. Acharya, Baburam, *Bada Maharajadhiraja Prithvinarayan Shah Ko Jeevani* (Biography of His Majesty's King Prithvinarayan Shah), First Edition, Kathmandu: Press Secretariate of His Majesty the King, 2024 B.S.
2. Bajracharya, Gautam Bajra, *Hanumandhoka Rajdarbar* (The Royal Palace Hanumandhoka) Kathmandu, Nepal and Asian Institute, T.U. 2033.
3. Bista, Dar Bahadur, *Sabai Jata ko Phulbari*, Kathmandu, Ratna Pustak Bhandar, 1972-80.
4. Dahal, Dilliram, *Dhimal Lok Jeevan*, Royal Nepal Academy, 2036.
5. Dibas, Tulas, *Pradarshankari Dhimal Jati ko Lok Sanskriti*, Royal Nepal Academy, 2035.
6. His Majesty's Government, Department of Communication and Information *Mechidekhi Mahakali* (Mechi to Mahakali) Part I, Kathmandu: Department of Information, HMG, Nepal 2031.
7. Sharma, Balchandra, *Nepal Ko Aitihasik Ruprekha* (The Outline History of Nepal), Fourth Edition, Baranasi, Krishna Kumari Devi 2033.
8. Sharma, Negendra, *Nepali Janajeeban* (Nepalese Lives) Darjeelling, Achalan Bhagawati Publication, 1966 A.D.

9. Shrestha, Bihari Krishna, *Karnali Lok Sanskriti* (Culture of Karnali) Part III, Kathmandu: Royal Nepal Academy 2028.
10. Shrestha, Swayambhu Lal, *Hamro Garima* (Our Pride), First Edition, Bhadrapur, Alok Press, 2032.
11. Shrestha, Swayambhu Lal, *Hami Nepali* (We Nepalese), First Edition, Lalitpur, Shrestha Publication, 2028.
12. Yogi, Narahari Nath, *Itihas Prakashma Sandhipatra Sangraha* (Collection of Treaties and Papers in Historical Background), Dang, 2032 B.S.

ENGLISH

1. B.S. Sir Edward, *Anthropology*, U.S.A., The University of Michigan Press, 1960.
2. Bista, Dor Bahadur, *People of Nepal*, Kathmadu, Ratna Pustak Bhandar, 2nd Edition, 1972.
3. Boas, Franz, *Baco Language and Culture*, New York, The Macmillan Company, 1969.
4. Crooks, W.B.A., *The Tribes and Castes of North Western India*, Vol. II, Cosmo Publication Delhi, Reprinted 1974.
5. Gautam Dr. Rajesh & Thapa, Ashok K., *Tribal Ethonography of Nepal*, Vol. I and II, India, Book Faith of India, 1994 A.D.
6. Furer, Haimondorfed, *Caste And Kim in Nepal, India and Ceylon*, London, Asia Publishing House, 1966.
7. Ghurye G.S., *Caste, Class and Occupation*, Bombay, Popular Book Depot.
8. Ghurye G.S., *Caste and Class in India*, Bombay, Popular Book Depot, 1957.
9. Hamilton, Francis Buchanan, *An Account of The Kingdom of Nepal*, New Delhi, Manjusri Publishing House, 1971.
10. Hodgson, Brain, *Miscellaneous Essays Relating To Indian Subject*, Vol. I, London, Trubnerco Ludgate Hill, 1880.
11. Hulton, J.H., *Caste In India*, Fourth Edition, Oxford University Press, 1963.
12. Karn, P.O., *Nepal : A Cultural and Physical Geography* Lemington, Kentucky, 1960.
13. Majumdar, D.N., *Races And Cultures of India*, Bombay, Asia Publishing House, 1961.
14. Old Field, B. Amirose, *Sketches From Nepal*, Vol. I, Delhi, Cosmo Publications, 1974.

15. Pomble, John, *The Invasion of Nepal*, World Clerendon Press, 1971.
16. Risley, Sir Herbert, *The People of India*, 2nd Edition, London W. Thacker and Co., 1915.
17. Sanyal, Charu Chandra, *The Rajbanshi's of North Bengal* (A Study of the Hindu Social Group), Calcutta, The Asiatic Society, 1965.
18. Stokin, J.S., *Social Anthropology*, New York, The Macmillan Company, 1950.

OTHERS

1. Journal
2. Census Report of Bengal, 1891
3. Census Report of Bengal, Vol. I, 1872.
4. Census Report of India, Vol. V, Part I, 1911.
5. Descriptive Ethnology of Bengal, 1872.
6. Journal of Asiatic Society of Bengal, Vol. XVIII, Part II, 1849.
7. Wild Tribes of India, 1882.

Pictorials

A Rajbanshi woman on a traditional "PETANI" dress.

A typical Rajbanshi family of eastern Nepal.

A mixture of traditional and modern thoughts.

An aspiring young Rajbanshi.

A temple belonging to the Rajbanshi's.

The worshipping place of the Rajbanshi's.

Goddess of the Rajbanshi's "DEVI KALI".

A Rajbanshi on Death rites (purification).